Editors: Angela K. Durden and Tom Whitfield
Cover design and interior layout: Angela K. Durden
www.angeladurden.com

BLUEROOMBOOKS.COM
blueroombooks@outlook.com
A MARINE and a JOURNALIST
WALK INTO A BAR
JEDWIN SMITH
978-1-950729-10-4

ISBN 13: 978-1-950729-10-4

Dedicated to all the editors through the years who had faith in my ability to get the story and in whose abilities I had faith to correct my shortcomings and make me look good.

It is you who won my awards for me.

To David —
The great stories
all come via the
hand of God —
Jedwin Smith
19 June 2021

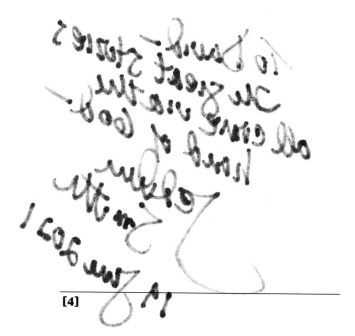

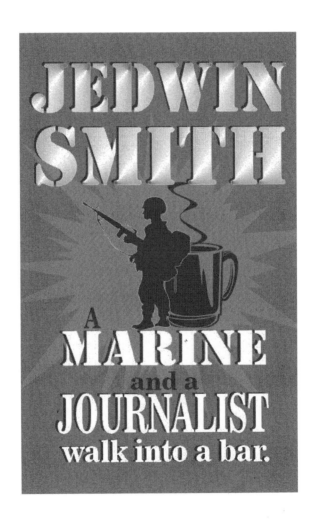

A Journalist and a Marine Walk Into a Bar

FOREWORD

"You want to hire the outdoors editor of the *Atlanta Journal-Constitution* to be the *Gwinnett Daily News* sports columnist?"

That was the reaction, topped with a large dose of incredulity, in April 1989 within the Atlanta sports community when this upstart suburban newspaper hired Jedwin Smith.

When word spread that the *Gwinnett Daily News*, owned by *The New York Times* and funded to compete with the venerable *AJC*, was looking for the right fit for this prestigious position, there were plenty of applicants with established resumes in sportswriting and columnizing vying for the job.

As the sports editor, it was my responsibility to present candidates to the editor and managing editor of the newspaper. We were in agreement on the job description: a person who not only would cover the whole gamut of

Atlanta area sports from professional to collegiate, but also would embrace high school and youth sports, all of which could help drive circulation.

There was only one person I wanted for this job and it was someone I had history with and thus knew what we were getting. He fit the description of a reporter all newspapers these days could do well to emulate:

A man of the people because he was the people. A man who would tirelessly represent the newspaper in the community and create a must-read following. A man who was an underdog, just like the rest of us at the *Gwinnett Daily News* who knew we had to be our best every day to prove we belonged in the Atlanta sports scene.

That man was Jedwin Smith.

We first met in 1976 when, as John Smith, he was named sports editor of the *Racine Journal-Times*, my Wisconsin hometown newspaper where I was employed as a sportswriter.

His writing heroes were George Plimpton and Hunter S. Thompson, kings of participatory and Gonzo journalism. He was never shy in regaling with stories of his life in the Marine Corps and stories he'd done. For instance, in Florida he got in the ring and went two quick rounds with light-heavyweight boxing contender Mike Quarry. That hysterical story is one of many included in this book.

Jedwin always had a nose for the story angle that regular folks, readers, would like to know about. Sometimes it seemed as if stories simply fell in his lap. (Hank Aaron knew about that.)

In addition to writing columns and interesting human interest feature stories in Racine, and winning numerous awards, John was an award-winning page designer, which led to stops at the *Chicago Tribune* and *Kansas City Times*. Unfortunately, the writing talent remained bottled as he designed more award-winning pages in Chicago and was sports editor in Kansas City, a non-writing position.

I had moved to the *Atlanta Constitution* in 1977 as sports editor. In 1981, John was hired by the *Atlanta Journal* (the *Journal* and *Constitution* editorial staffs merged in 1982) where he was Sunday sports editor, another frustrating non-writing position.

The lifestyle of a newspaper page designer and section editor is not conducive to good health, what with the long hours and working nights and weekends. Tense and taut deadlines as well as personal demons brought pressures that needed relieving. It all caught up to him in late 1982 and early 1983. He spent three months in an alcohol rehabilitation center to get a handle on that.

Returning to the newspaper, he was moved out of the high-pressure sports department setting into the low-key lifestyle department, again not writing.

But not for long.

When more than 200 U.S. Marines were killed Oct. 23, 1983, in a terrorist truck bombing in Beirut, it lit a fire under the ex-Marine. He stormed into the managing editor's office and said "I'm either going over there to fight or report on the situation."

Two weeks later he and a staff photographer were embedded with U.S. troops, which lasted months. He was writing again and his big story of "Christmas in a combat zone" — the Marines' first big test since Vietnam — was nominated for a Pulitzer Prize.

Only his stories were not bylined by John Smith. The newspaper hierarchy, thinking John Smith too common, made it J. Edwin Smith, using first initial and then his middle name.

So, how does one become a Jedwin?

About that time *Return of the Jedi* was the latest in the *Star Wars* series. Thus, when J. Edwin Smith returned to the newspaper offices on Jan. 7, 1984, I yelled out "It's the Return of the Jedwin" as his co-workers stood and applauded the bravado it took for him to report from a war zone.

Being a Pulitzer nominee was lost on the newspaper management and Jedwin was returned to the sports department, sentenced to life as the outdoors editor. However, he did talk his way into writing about local Ducks Unlimited hunters who won a fishing trip to the Florida Keys, and on that trip — always finding gold in an assignment — he came across Mel Fisher's treasure salvors discovering the *Atocha*, one of the lost Spanish treasure galleons. That story graced the *AJC* pages. He later wrote *Fatal Treasure*, a book-length telling of the adventure of living and diving with the crew and being there when the treasure was found.

Upon his return, his reward for writing these interesting reader-favorite stories was to again be banished to designing *Atlanta Journal* editions on the overnight shift...

...until February 1986.

The Foreign Desk editor called him over. "Is your passport in order? Still up to date?" Affirmative. "How would you like to go to East Africa?"

So this rebel with a cause, who would do anything to get out of designing pages, was off to East Africa for several months, covering the Eritrea-Ethiopia civil war. The hook was that the Morehouse School of Medicine (based in Atlanta) was donating life-saving antibiotics and vitamins. Jedwin would accompany the shipment and report on their effect among the ravaged Eritrean population.

The stories were in a special section that was a Pulitzer finalist.

Again, his reward?

Back to designing pages and later outdoors editor. He never did write mainstream sports at the *AJC*.

But I knew what he had written in Belvidere, Illinois, where he had lived as a teen and had begun his career as a one-man sports staff, then in Florida and Racine, and the touching stories in Beirut and Africa.

When it came time to meet the *Gwinnett Daily News* editor and managing editor, he presented them with three sports columns that he did on his own in the Atlanta area and a list of 100 column ideas.

He was hired as Jedwin Smith.

He wrote from the heart.

It was spending an hour with Willie Nelson on his tour bus to write about Willie Nelson, Sports Fan.

It was bonding with Falcons coach Jerry Glanville, one of the true characters in the world of sports.

It was chronicling the Atlanta Braves' run to glory in 1991 and '92.

It was the day he was watching his 10-year-old daughter play softball, and a physically challenged player on the opposing team got the first hit of her career, which prompted players and fans from both teams to rush to her side on the basepath in celebration. His column describing that event brought tears to many, many eyes.

It was setting up "Hey, Jedwin", the forerunner of today's chats in which fans would leave questions on an answering machine and Jedwin would reply in once-a-week columns.

He was a man for all seasons and all reasons. Always the underestimated talent because he didn't care so much for the glory accruing to him if to get that glory he couldn't tell the story that needed telling. He hated spin, and climbing ladders to nowhere held no fascination for him.

The reply to "You want to hire the outdoors editor of the *Atlanta Journal-Constitution* to be the *Gwinnett Daily News* sports columnist?" lies in the 56 writing awards he's won, most of them while at the *Daily News*.

We called our work at the *Daily News* the best job we ever had. Sadly, the last edition rolled off the press on Sept. 6, 1992. The *AJC* bought us out and shut us down to remove the growing threat in the Atlanta market. We were all out of work. Jedwin was down to his last $2.37 when the *AJC* called to offer him a part-time job designing pages. He was told in no uncertain terms that he would not be writing. He eventually was promoted to full time, which lasted until 2007 when he retired.

We all were on the rebound after the *AJC* bought out the *GDN*. I moved on to Rochester, N.Y., as assistant managing editor for sports, then back to the *AJC* as an editor in the sports department from 1994-96. When CNN merged with Time-Warner in 1996, a new cable TV 24-hour sports news network was launched, CNN/Sports Illustrated; they recruited me to be its senior editor. That lasted until May 2002, when the channel was shut down for lack of distribution. I then moved on to MLB Advanced Media, Major League Baseball's internet arm known as MLB.com, where I was an editor until the 2020 pandemic hit.

I had the privilege of working with many extremely talented people at all those stops, and the preceding locales in my career. I can honestly say John/J. Edwin/Jedwin Smith is the best teammate I've ever had.

Enjoy these stories behind the stories from a true soldier of fortune.

Paul Bodi

On the last day of 2020
The guy who knew Jedwin back when he was plain old John Smith.

Paul Bodi
and The Drunk

2020

Priming the Pump

Only now, at 74, is it all making sense. I write this introduction at the end of a tough three weeks.

Amid a flood of prayers from family and friends, my brother Joe slipped into a coma and on into death, dying on March 4, 2020. A great friend of mine, Philip Haney, fighting on the side of right against dark forces both at home and abroad, was murdered in California two weeks earlier by enemies of Truth and Good.

Then Steve Klink, a fellow Marine who was with my brother Jeff in 'Nam and instrumental in my writing the family memoir *Our Brother's Keeper*, called to say cancer was slowly eating away his innards. He didn't have long. Ivy, another buddy and 'Nam vet who lived across the street from me, died.

Gil, my daughter Jill's 84-year-old father-in-law, died of bone cancer two weeks before.

Our old enemy, the grave, was visiting me right and left. Dammit — just doesn't seem fair. Even though I'm an author of Irish lineage, meaning you must muzzle me to stop me from going on and on with my blessed gift for storytelling, I've never known what to say when confronted with death.

I'll say that I'm sorry, but then lapse into tongue-tied silence.

Whatever regrets I'm feeling have always been easier to share in front of a computer, stoically silent as fingers are whaling away at a keyboard, but crying on the inside.

I remember Dad always bitching about old age, how he was tired of idly sitting by as friends and family died before him. There is a correlation between the accumulation of wisdom and advancing age.

So now, as the shadow of death creeps closer and closer to me, I'm sitting here in quiet solitude looking over my shoulder, thinking about all those yesterdays. Sometimes with a self-serving smirk, but mostly realizing God has spent a lot of time intervening on my behalf, protecting me from myself even as my faith in Him vacillated.

So, anyway, here I am. An old man leafing through old scrapbooks and clip files and photographs. Thumbing through my journalistic career, one that spanned 36 years and nine newspapers en route to winning 56 major writing awards, including twice being nominated for the Pulitzer Prize — the print media's equivalent to an Oscar.

You might think, given my temper and alcoholism, that I had a hard time holding onto a job. Just the opposite was true, though. I overcame those negatives by simply outworking the other dudes.

I passed through one state after another in a drunken flurry, always to the backdrop of a country song — Illinois to Florida, then off to Wisconsin before landing at the *Chicago Tribune*, which I left in a huff toward the Kansas-Missouri border, then off to Georgia's *Atlanta Journal-Constitution* and sobriety, next shifting across town to the *Gwinnett Daily News* (enjoying the greatest three years of my journalistic life, kicking ass and taking names), and finally meekly returning to the *Atlanta Journal-Constitution* after it purchased the *Daily News* and locked its doors.

Anyway, I've always managed to keep smiling. And hopefully you, too, can share a few smiles with me as I steer you down an aging writer's memory lane with short stories and anecdotes — not to mention a bit of Looney Tunes madness — that spans the better part of 50 years.

Along the way, this wannabe cowboy will take you into professional sports clubhouses, locker rooms, dorm rooms, batting cages, dugouts, infields, outfields, trains, planes, automobiles, and motorbikes.

You can also accompany me into Willie Nelson's private motorhome as I share fried chicken and our love of sports with the Red Headed Stranger.

You can share a ride with NFL Falcons coach Jerry Glanville on his Harley and see legendary Falcons coach Norm Van Brocklin threaten to kick my ass when I ask pointed questions about another lackluster loss.

You can climb into the ring as I trade punches with light-heavyweight contender Mike Quarry; and compare scars with motorcycle daredevil Evel Knievel; and many more.

It's been one helluva journey. These are the backstories to the columns and interviews that made it into the papers and some books. Funny thing, though, is this: I'm sleeping so much better. The bad dreams are not nearly as frequent. I always thought of revisiting my life as a dredging operation — dirty, muddy, and not a bit of fun. But of all things, this walk of mine down memories' lanes has turned into something more akin to tending a garden and plucking the beautiful fruits and vegetables.

Another writer said in Ecclesiastes 2:24 that a man should see good for his hard work. In writing this book I am focusing on all that good in my hard work. And maybe, just maybe, that is what my God has been trying to teach me all along.

Jedwin Smith

At home in his basement office

March 8, 2020

Just as The Great Coronavirus Shutdown began. And if such a time as this ain't the right time to be writing a damn book, then there just ain't no right time to be writing a damn book.

POSTSCRIPT

December 22, 2020

As I sit with my editor putting in pictures for the book, I can't help but remember my friend Steve Klink, who passed away just two weeks ago. It was he who put me in touch with all the Marines who survived when Jeff was killed during the Tet Offensive and that led to the writing of *Our Brother's Keeper*. A piece of me died when his wife, Joy, told me the sad news.

A Journalist and a Marine Walk Into a Bar

1964

The Tale of an Indentured Marine

Marine Corps Recruit Depot-San Diego. We're talking ancient history. Pat Boone was still relevant, as were LBJ, cigarettes, and drive-in theaters.

It was June 1964 and five dozen or so of us teenage misfits were suffering through our initial days of boot camp, which was as close to a thirteen-week stint in Hell as any of us had yet ever experienced. Vietnam was still two years distant.

Our DI (drill instructor) — half-Puerto Rican, half-Neanderthal — rarely spoke. He mostly screamed, constantly reminding us we were "raggedy-assed" handfuls of human excrement. Depending on the day of the week, we were a friggin' mob, maggots, or motherless scum. Individually, we were called "boots".

Our days began in darkness at 0530 and concluded in collapsed "lights out" exhaustion at 2200 hours. And during the nine-hundred-ninety minutes in between we ran and did everything else by the numbers — pushups, squat thrusts, chin-ups — and then we ran some more. To break the monotony, we learned the intricacies of our M-14 rifles, the legendary history of the Corps, and mastered close-order drill on a blacktopped quadrant called The Grinder.

We ate together, hit the head together, ran together, and marched together. Everything in unison. Teamwork the order of the day. No room for individualism. The Corps eliminated our independence and rebuilt us to its Gung Ho specs; no longer did we take time to think about the pros and cons of any and all situations — instead, we did as ordered.

Without question.

Ours was a joyless environment. But at the end of the tunnel — after ninety-one days of near-insanity that chiseled us into lean, mean fighting machines — were those awesome dress blues. Lady magnets if there ever was one.

Boot camp instilled in us a new language. I'm not referring to swearing, although a Marine's coarse vocabulary is legendary.

A wall was not a wall, but a bulkhead. Ditto a toilet, which was a head. The floor was the deck, which we hit with monotonous regularity — daily pushups by the hundreds. We didn't wear hats, we wore covers. Pants were what women wore; we wore trousers.

We didn't dine in a cafeteria; we chowed down in a mess hall. We didn't sleep in a bed; we grunts sacked out in the rack.

For entertainment, we fought each other — under strict supervision, however. With padded clubs, hand-to-hand tactics, simulated bayonet drills. We smaller boots were always paired against the bigger dudes in order to pummel the fear-factor out of us.

Those who wavered, who never could quite get with the program, were a detriment to us all. If one boot screwed up, the entire platoon paid the price, usually with seemingly endless pushups. Or, worse yet, our "smoking lamp" would be canceled.

Indeed, we came to believe that somewhere in that "Guidebook for Marines" that we lived by it said cigarette depredation helped build teamwork.

A boot would drop his rifle, God help him. Or briefly stand under the shower spigot and refuse to apply soap. Or maybe his foot locker wasn't in proper order. The infractions were mind-numbing, the punishment soul-sapping. You either learned quickly or...well, the DI would call us to attention and, in a thundering voice, ask, "So, maggots, what the hell are we gonna do about that shitbird?"

In one instance, I took matters into my own hands. Truth be known, it haunts me to this day, although...

I remember him as Lush-shiana, the hyphen meaning he slurred much of his speech. He was a massive, big-boned kid. A swamp critter born down on the bayou. A Purple Tiger fan of Louisiana State University, always rattling on about Billy Cannon. Anyway, the dude's slurring was due to a mouthful of bad teeth. No, I take that back; he had a mouthful of rotten teeth. Which I had no way of knowing at the time until that fateful early-morning moment during our eighth or ninth day in Hell.

Out there on The Grinder, asshole to belly button, running in lock-step — left, right, left, by the numbers. All of us scared shitless, fearing the wrath of our DI for some real or imagined screw-up.

Besides being born with two left feet, Lush-shiana also had the IQ of a squirrel. You have to understand that, until the advent of today's computerized battlefield, the Corps wasn't looking to recruit Rhodes Scholars. They wanted knuckleheads they could convince to willingly charge enemy machine-gun emplacements. Dudes who idolized John Wayne, he of Sgt. Stryker fame in the movie *Sands of Iwo Jima*. Hooligans who would kill for the honor of being a Marine.

Most of us fit the bill. The majority could read and write and had had our difficulties at home and with the police. Above all else, most of us joined for the opportunity to legally break things and hurt people. And get paid to do it.

What a deal, huh?

Lush-shiana, however, was…well, in today's parlance, he was problematic. Back in the day I swore he was mentally deficient — constantly confused, especially when it came to telling his left foot from his right. Which is hell on wheels when it comes to running in lock-step formation. Especially when Lush-shiana was plodding along, directly behind me.

And forever stepping on my heels.

Clomp!

And I almost fell on my face, falling into the boot in front of me, who screamed, "Bust that bastard."

Clomp!

Tripped up again, this time yelling to Lush-shiana to get in step.

But he didn't, instead nailing my heel again, sending me stumbling forward. Which prompted the dude in front of me to fire an elbow into my chest. Quick-tempered in those days, I spun around and fired a straight right fist into Lush-shiana's mouth.

This, followed by a scream from the galoot and what seemed like a geyser of blood and teeth.

Gee-zus! Then all hell broke loose.

Lush-shiana dropped to his knees, taking a couple of stumbling boots with him. Chaos as the platoon broke ranks, and our DI going ballistic: "What the fuck's goin' on here? Whoa, herd. Smith, what the hell happened, you turd?"

Long story short, ol' Lush-shiana was hustled off to sick call, where Navy corpsmen did their best to clean up his wound, and then days later the DI informed us that the Navy dental folks were addressing the lad's problem. With no further explanation forthcoming, the smoking lamp was lit. And from that moment on, the rest of the boots gave me a wide berth.

Hell, I felt like John Wayne himself.

I was bulletproof.

Invincible.

The DI appointed me squad leader.

Problem was, Lush-shiana would soon be rejoining the platoon, which I dreaded. This big-boned, swamp-raised critter probably wrestled gators back home in his spare time. In a fair fight, he'd kick the shit out of me. So all I could do was fret about his return, get my affairs in order, and await Armageddon.

And then, several days later, here he came. His shadow darkening Platoon Street. Godzilla blocking out the sun. A-runnin' toward us, his big-booted feet actually working in synch, his immensely muscled arms a-flyin', and his steely eyes afire.

Admittedly, confusion set in at this point. In my mind's eye, I saw my mother back home lighting a candle in church for the redemption of my soul. All the while I'm praying for forgiveness of my sins: *Hail Mary, full of grace, pray for us sinners*...as I rigidly awaited a greatly-deserved ass-kicking.

But no way was I going down without a fight. With fists clenched, I stared down the enemy, just like John Wayne did on those fabled Iwo Jima sands. By God, I, too, was going to die with my boots on.

And just like that, in the blink of an eye — no, in the magnanimous flash of a wide-mouthed toothy grin — ol' Lush-shiana wrapped me in a bone-crushing hug and shouted over and over: "Thank you, thank you, I'm a-thankin' you..."

That Louisiana swamp dweller had been plagued by bad teeth all his short-lived life. "Bad tooths and gum ailments, no end in sight," he said. "And then youse hep'd me out, me gettin' to dem dentist folk 'hed o' schedule. Deys jerked out the rest o' 'ems bad'ens an' gives me a new mouthfuls of tooths."

To prove the point, he grabbed me by the shoulders and jaw-jutted a pristine mouthful of dentures before my startled eyes. "Jes looky here, sees for yuz'selfs. So's I's a-thankin' you. Can't thanks you 'nuff," he said, releasing his fearsome grip.

With a straight face, I said, "Ah…my pleasure, Boot."

Never did call him Lush-shiana again. Which is how I lived to fight another day.

1971

Going Weird, Going Pro

It was late December 1970. I was 25, honorably discharged from the Marine Corps, married with a one-year-old daughter, and struggling through my senior year at Northern Illinois University, working on a B.A. in journalism. Struggling because, even though I was only six hours short of graduation, newspaper jobs were in short supply. Other than my family, I had two passions in life — the Corps and writing about sports.

The Corps was no longer an option. Hated life as a mushroom, being kept in the dark and fed only horseshit. Not knowing what might be lying in wait around the next bend in the road irritated the hell out of me. Needing to unwind, I made the half-hour drive from the NIU campus in DeKalb to Belvidere, where my mother and four siblings lived.

Didn't stop at home right away. Instead, I parked the car downtown and walked into a bar.

Funny how things turn out.

I'd never met Bill Hetland, a U.S. Army dude who'd just returned home from active duty in Vietnam. When I walked into Dodge Lanes on that wintry December evening, I spotted him decked out in full dress uniform, sitting directly across from me at the big horseshoe bar. Do believe he was imbibing a rum-and-grape-soda concoction — a Vietnam delicacy.

It was his Big Red One division patch that first caught my attention. Jarheads get a militaristic kick out of ribbing "doggies", and vice versa. He kept repeating his division's mantra: "If you're gonna be one, be a Big Red One." Can't remember my response, but I'm sure it's not fit for family consumption. Hetland gave as good as he got. Once a ceasefire was declared, we shook hands and drank away the rest of the night.

What I didn't know was Hetland had just accepted an offer to become the *Belvidere Daily Republican's* managing editor. He was a journalism graduate of nearby Northern Illinois University. Said he knew my wife, June, who was an off-campus hair stylist.

Oh, yeah? I bristled.

"Yeah, her and my brother, Rich, are close friends," Hetland said. "They were Homecoming King and Queen. You know, Class of '65."

Okaaaaaay. He ordered another round, and our conversation continued. Peacefully.

Somewhere during our "Welcome Home, Bro" alcoholic soiree, Hetland said he'd heard through the NIU grapevine that I was a sports columnist at the NIU student newspaper; a controversial columnist, at that. Greatly read and greatly criticized, he joked. And poorly reimbursed for the aggravation. He'd also worked at the student newspaper before joining the Army and being shipped off to 'Nam.

Long story short, Hetland hired me a week or so later as the BDR's sports editor. I was now head of the one-man sports staff, which meant I was my own boss...well, almost. Hetland knew I was a fan of Hunter S. Thompson and George Plimpton — the former a certified whacko who embraced Gonzo journalism in *Rolling Stone* magazine, the latter the master of "participatory journalism", always personally injecting himself into the stories he covered. Thompson always fighting Big Brother in print, the master of "Fear and Loathing" in whatever zipped through his splintered schizoid personality; Plimpton climbing into the ring against heavyweight legend Archie Moore or participating in NFL training camp as the Detroit Lions' backup quarterback, in both instances getting thoroughly whacked.

Anyway, having heard of my reporting antics at NIU, Hetland thought it wise for me to take a psychological test. "Nothing of the sort like in the [1962] novel *One Flew Over the Cuckoo's Nest,* by Ken Kesey," Hetland assured me. I had no idea to what he was referring. My reading tastes centered on military history, Thompson,

and Plimpton. "This test evaluates...
uhhh, you know...your strengths."

I took the test and waited for the
results. Can't remember when Hetland
shared them with me, but I'm sure it
was over drinks.

Estimated Intelligence: Superior.

Energy Potential: Works hard when
he can see immediate personal
results.

**Thoroughness/Ability to Handle
Details:** Handles details
adequately but is rather
impatient with paperwork.

Initiative/Willingness to Work: Is
somewhat individualistic and apt
to do things his own way.

Aggressiveness: Strong and
vigorous, quite outgoing, will
take chances.

Test's conclusions: His attitude may
hinder his rate of growth; Is a
rather impatient and brash young

man; Is apt to take on the world on issues that appeal to him; Can see things in new and different ways; Is ambitious and is out to prove he is the best; Needs a superior who will be willing to back him when he is right but also to slow him down when he is being impetuous.

Viewing the psycho test results almost a half-century later, it had me pegged correctly. As for Hetland, he proved to be one of the greatest and most innovative bosses of all.

Steppingstones to bigger venues meant covering the local high school sports scene, plus junior tackle football, Colt League baseball, various bowling leagues, and whatever else cropped up within the limited confines of *Belvidere Daily Republican's* (*BDR*) 6000-plus circulation area. Advancing higher in journalism's food chain to bigger assignments at more prestigious newspapers is a matter of patience, not to mention acquiring advanced writing skills and contacts.

Honing my craft *patiently* was difficult. I wanted to be Howard Cosell *right now*. I wanted to interview Joe Namath and Paul Hornung plus my all-time heroes Ernie Banks and Billy Martin *right now.* Bragging to my kids that once upon a time I'd interviewed Jimmy-high-school-sports-star just wasn't going to cut it, but players from the two-time Super Bowl champion Green Bay Packers? Oh, yeah, telling that to the kids would cut it.

So it was that my impatience got the better of me.

One of my literary heroes, Hunter S. Thompson, said, "When the going gets weird, the weird turn pro." I embraced that ethos and contacted the Packers' PR department, introduced myself, and asked if I could get press credentials to cover their Sunday, July 19, Press Picture Day in Green Bay. Packers PR said "You betcha! No sweat!"

Even Bill Hetland was excited about the prospect. After all, the *BDR* didn't publish on Sunday, so we weren't on the company's dime. He grabbed his camera, offered to drive, and away we went. Big shots from a tiny town of 12,000, en route to the NFL Promised Land. Well, almost…

The once-great Packers had stumbled upon hard times, no longer the league's dominating power of the 1960s. Vince Lombardi had moved on to coach the Washington Redskins, dying in 1970; Green Bay's once-vibrant stars of yesteryear were showing their age.

Not that any of this mattered because Bill and I felt bulletproof — we were steppin' on out.

Four hours and 230 miles later, despite the threat of rain, we were in NFL Nirvana, joining a scrum of fellow sportswriters huddled around future Hall of Fame quarterback Bart Starr, twice the MVP of the AFL-NFL World Championship. The term "Super Bowl" hadn't yet come into play.

Anyway, the rest of the media mob had come prepared with tape recorders — and umbrellas. The Corps issued ponchos so, hell, I'd never used an umbrella in my life. Tape recorders cost a small fortune; a buck-fifty a week salary did not support that expenditure. I relied on the old standby — ink pen and a reporter's notebook. Hetland snapped pictures.

About 10 minutes into Starr's give-and-take with reporters, it started to rain. Lightly, but without letup. Starr, always the consummate gentleman, continued for a short while, then said, "Sorry, guys, but I gotta run."

When I stepped aside to let him through, he noticed everything I'd jotted down in my notebook was obliterated by the rain.

He hesitated, waiting for the rest of the media to clear out, then laid his hand on my shoulder and motioned to his station wagon parked nearby and said, "Why don't we continue this over there."

Don't know about Hetland, but I floated over to Starr's vehicle. I was pinching myself and screaming inside: "My God, is this really happening?"

Indeed, it was.

Numb with excitement, Hetland was in the back seat listening in to me in the front. And for the next thirty minutes, the game's classiest act patiently and

politely answered all my questions —
not once viewing my professional
standing as suspect; instead, treating me
as if I was a well-known, big-time
reporter. The rain ceased shortly before
the interview was concluded, at which
time Starr grabbed the football lying in
the gap between us, and then motioned
for me to join him on the sidelines,
where the league's official staff
photographers would snap pictures.

Bart Starr wanted me to play catch
with him? Whoa. The little kid in me
almost wet his pants as I trotted 20
yards away, turned dramatically, and
nervously awaited the greatest gift of a
lifetime. Awaiting that first pass found
me daydreaming.

*It's January 15, 1967, in Memorial
Stadium in Los Angeles; and it's me (not
Max McGee) cutting left to right over the
middle, reaching behind me with my right*

hand to haul in Starr's slightly off-target
pass, then scampering into the end zone for
a 37-yard touchdown — scoring the first
TD in Super Bowl history. Immortalized,
forever.

But then reality knocked.

Starr cocked his arm and lofted the ball to me…a perfect spiral, right in the numbers.

The cameras clicked, capturing all…

The ball sails into my hands and…

THUNK!

Ricocheted off my chest and onto the ground. Yikes, I'd muffed it. Felt like dying. Instead of glory, I'd failed in my first 15 seconds of fame.

Not that it bothered Starr, however. Smiling all the while, he motioned for me to pick up the ball and toss it back to him. We continued, back and forth, until the cameras stopped clicking. I enthusiastically thanked Bart, then went in search of Packer Coach Dan Devine, Ray Nitschke, and Mike McCoy, all of whom also graced me with interviews.

And Bill Hetland, grinning ear to ear, didn't stop snapping pics.

The four-hour return to Belvidere that afternoon passed quickly.

My mind replaying what, to this day, I still consider to be a dream-come-true event, rubbing shoulders with the game's elite. And best of all, playing catch with Bart Starr.

Damn, life was good!

Mike McCoy

Who's that little boy in the
striped pants begging for an autograph?

Dan Devine

Two weeks later our four-part series on the Packers caused a shitstorm. Phones at the *BDR* rang off the hook. Belvidere's Chicago Bears faithful were pissed. All calls had the same tone and message: "What the hell's this Packer garbage, Smith? You're in Illinois, boy — this is (bleepin') Bears Country."

Last thing Hetland wanted was another war on his hands. 'Nam had been enough. But a full-fledged riot in his hometown was another matter. He huddled with associate publisher Pat Mattison, and before you could say "the Bears suck" — which they had for the previous eight seasons — I was given the thumbs-up to venture to Rensselaer, Indiana, where the Bears conducted their training camp on the St. Joseph's College campus.

Time was of the essence. We gotta do it now, meaning yesterday, and it was already High Noon on Friday, August 6.

Did as much advance work as possible on Saturday's edition, then turned the rest over to Hetland. He was quite adept at juggling three grenades.

Getting to Rensselaer was gonna be problematic — Chicago traffic, in and out of the city, meant at least a three-hour battle south to the St. Joe campus. Made the trip with Hetland's twisted humor ringing in my ear: "What's it you grunts say? Adapt, Improvise, Overcome. Right? So, come back with a four-part series, bucko!"

Arrived at dusk. Had no idea what the protocol was other than I'd be bedding down at a brown-brick student dormitory called Justin Hall. The dorm receptionist would have a room key waiting for me. Managed to locate the dorm, but the receptionist, a bespectacled college kid, had no idea which specific rooms the players were staying in. Said, "Just knock on any second-floor door, I guess; that's where they're bunking down."

Took him at his word yet couldn't find a Bears PR man to save my soul. Undaunted, I found a nearby parking spot, grabbed my gym bag and camera gear, and sprinted back to the building. Through the glass door, found my first-floor room and dumped my gear, then jogged up a flight of stairs, and came to the nearest three doors.

Decisions, decisions. So, I played like Monty Hall of *Let's Make a Deal* fame. Briefly hesitated, then chose Door Number Two.

Timidly knocked. A tired, gravelly voice responded: "Entah, brothah."

Obeyed and was confronted by two monumental, yet horizontal Bears, each reclining with their size thirteen feet dangling over the front of their way-too-small twin beds. Black dudes.

Am sure I was bug-eyed because I had no idea who they were. Instantly realized I'd just stepped into Rookie Reporter Hell. Mind racing, but before I could respond, the Bear closest to the door said, "My, my — lookey here, Counselor. Do believe it be a membah of the Fourth Estate."

I stammered once. Then again. Finally got the words out, identifying myself in a halting, if not rambling voice, admitting this was my first introduction to the Bears and...well, dammit, I hadn't yet received a press guide with individual player profiles and pictures, so pled ignorance because "I have no idea who you dudes are...ah, but if I gotta fight in the next war, I'd certainly be honored to have both of you on my side."

An uncomfortable silence stretched long like a Bear fan waiting on his prayers to be answered.

Then big grins because it was obvious they were enjoying my extreme discomfort. Probably wondering which of the nearby Indiana villages was missing its idiot.

Found my tongue again. Said, "Ah, sorry for barging in like this, guys, but I sure am hopin' y'all could spare me a few moments of your time because I've gotta head back home Sunday morning with enough interviews…"

Funny, how equal parts humility and admitted stupidity can break the ice. My anxiety turned into a half-hour or so of "Let's shuck and jive the Newbie Sportswriter", courtesy of defensive bookends George Seals and his mild-mannered sidekick, Willie Holman.

Seals, a glib six-three, 260 tackle, started the monologue by throwing out one cliché after another, laughing all the while. Began with the old standby that all NFL teams were equal talent-wise yet winning came down to which team was the hungriest, etcetera, etcetera, etcetera. Would have been bored to death had not Seals' banter been reminiscent of comedian Flip Wilson.

"What you gotta understand…John, right?" Seals asked.

I nodded in the affirmative.

"Cool. You see, John, all I want to know is if you're diggin' me. I mean, people must learn to communicate in order to survive in this cold, gray world. The game's all about defense, baby. And the Counselor and I play defense, which pleases us greatly because we get to hit people. We get to lash out and knock other people down."

He paused for dramatic effect, then said, "And knockin' people down is what we do best."

Seals paused, followed by another captivating grin, and then said, "Now, if you're lookin' for a sterling piece of wisdom from ol' George here, I'd say, to be honest, I think the Bears are going all the way. In fact, I'm optimistic as hell — and so is everyone else."

Seals looked across the room, where six-four, 250-pound defensive end Willie Holman reclined. Couldn't help but think about that earlier "hungriest team" chunk of wisdom. Seeking a second opinion, Seals asked, "What about that, Counselor? Am I layin' it on a bit too heavy?"

Holman was stoic, the straight man of the duo; he seemed as if he'd rather sleep than engage in idle conversation. Pondered the question for a beat or two, then finally said, "Heavy, George? Yes, it's heavy — but true. We're gonna go all the way to the top."

Spent another 20 minutes or so, thoroughly enjoying the banter — knowing the Bears, as usual, were short

on offensive might but always giving
their long-suffering fans enough
thunder and awe on the defensive side
of the line to keep the faithful coming
back. A run-of-the-mill franchise, yes.
But the only game in town. So, I played
along. And had fun doing so.

Finally, knowing I had enough for at
least one readable story, I thanked them
for taking the time to make this
neophyte feel at home. Seals nodded his
appreciation, then rose and stuck out his
huge hand. We exchanged a soul-
brother handshake…surprising him.

"Say, Counselor, ol-buddy John here
must have some black friends back
home," he said with a touch of
admiration. Smiled back at him and
asked for one last favor: "Maybe y'all
could spread the word tomorrow that
I'm not quite as stupid as I look, okay?"

Both got a kick out of that. And true
to their word, George Seals and Willie

Holman continued having fun at my expense the following morning and afternoon. It was a fair tradeoff. A few laughs in exchange for more stories.

Never did get a chance to speak with the Bears' head coach. I didn't even know his name. It was Seals who shook his head in disbelief, informing me it was Jim Dooley. Which prompted me to jokingly say, "Hey, didn't the Kingston Trio record a song about him?"

Not that it mattered. Dooley was fired seven months later after the Bears concluded another dismal 6-8 season.

Made the drive home Sunday with everything I needed to keep the Bears' Belvidere Faithful from getting restless. Also knew that, as far as reporting on professional sports was concerned, I'd been way over my head in Rensselaer. I'd have to curb my enthusiasm as well as my impatience. Without a doubt, quick advancement to the Big City and a higher-paying, more prestigious job would take several more years of hard work — and more hands-on education.

Despite my obvious weirdness, there was more to learn before going pro.

1972

An Ass-Kickin' and a Head-Scalpin'

Summer 1972. I'd been at the paper for a year now and approached Hetland with a Plimpton-esque idea of my getting into an argument (in print, of course) with Belvidere High Coach Doug Chapman about the school's lackluster football legacy. Belvidere's last great team was 25 years earlier, in 1947, which went 8-0. Since then the school had produced nothing close to that perfection. Those teams couldn't spell GREAT if spotted a G and T.

Chapman was in his third year at the helm. His first year, the Buccaneers were 0-9. In 1971, my first year on the job, the team stumbled to a 3-4-2 won-lost-tied record, yet I'd seen its potential. So had Chapman. There were studs galore — big-muscled dudes with speed. The team's only shortcomings were attitude and self-confidence. Too often they were beat before the opening kickoff. Peering across the field into a sea of black faces, they felt they could not possibly measure up to those oftentimes taller, bigger-boned speedsters.

Because my father was a school-teacher, his weekly paycheck was barely enough to make ends meet for a family of eight; we were Irish American gypsies. Dad repeatedly moved us onward and upward from one school and city to another, for 10-dollar-per-week raises.

Seven relocations in 11 years. It wasn't easy.

So it was that in my senior year we moved from Kewanee (in central Illinois) to Belvidere (northwest of Chicago) in mid-August 1963. Didn't bother me much, for I viewed the community the same way I had all the previous temporary ports of call — happiness would be Belvidere in my rearview mirror because I'd be enlisting in the Marine Corps upon graduation, a Smith family tradition.

So here I am in Belvidere but I felt like I'd just been transferred to apartheid South Africa. I was stunned. As a stud quarterback, I surveyed my Buccaneer teammates on the first day of practice. "Where the hell are the brothers?" I shouted.

In response, a solid mass of lily-white faces stared back, baffled. No blacks, no Chicanos. No transplanted

Poles or Eastern European welders, iron workers, or bricklayers. In other words, no street fighters who'd rather die than surrender. Crap. This new team was doomed — and in my senior year at that. Our family had moved to *Leave It to Beaver*-land.

During practice, I'd fire a pass to the precise spot a receiver was *supposed* to make the cut. But the ball careened off the back of his helmet because he'd failed to run the route correctly. So, did the errant receiver charge at me with fists a-flyin'? Hell no. He simply gave me a dirty look. That told me all I needed to know about his mental and physical toughness. We weren't winning with the likes of him.

Ended up dislocating my left shoulder in practice, missing three or four weeks of the regular season, and, due to the obvious lack of mobility and dexterity with a bulky, metal-and-leather shoulder brace, could no longer quarterback. Ended up playing defensive cornerback the rest of the way, using my head and right shoulder to spear opposing running backs.

Happiness was knocking someone on his ass.

Anyway, the season was a mediocre 4-4-1. Yes, that team had a handful of studs — Gary Gamlin, Don Pearson, Wes Dobbins, Rich Hetland, Dave Swanson, and Gary Pluff. But not enough to write home about. Far too many holes in our lineup and not nearly enough knuckle-draggers.

Got the picture? Okay. Moving forward to that 1972 rendition of Belvidere's football Bucs, I remember a conversation I'd had with Coach Chapman the year before. "When I first came to Belvidere," he said, "everyone warned me that Belvidere kids tended to cringe when they saw Rockford on the shirts of opposing players. I heard this again and again, even from Rockford coaches."

Chapman was stepping lightly around the racial question, the Big White Elephant cruising around the Belvidere High campus. Rockford, just up the road, was a bustling blue-collar manufacturing community, racially diverse with hungry, stone-cold thugs.

So, when Hetland and I were both at the paper and the school team was still not doing well, the idea I presented to him was this: Concoct a fictional confrontation with the Bucs' short-haired, establishment coaching staff and rile everybody up.

You see, they were always kidding me about my shoulder-length hair and wondering when I was going to man-up and get a real haircut, i.e. go high and tight with a crewcut. Despite the community's confidence that "this was the year the Bucs would attain greatness", I told Hetland I could write a story about how I was absolutely dreading covering this '72 team because I was convinced it would once again willfully surrender to the opposition — gutless and spineless, as always.

Way I looked at it, coaches could only do so much. Chapman's boys needed a verbal kick in the ass. They *needed* someone to *hate*. Someone tangible that could provoke them to "take a bullet for each other" week in and week out throughout a nine-game season. Someone to wake up their pride and honor.

What Marines call *esprit de corps*.

Hetland loved the idea. "You're saying the team needs something to incentivize them, right?"

Had no idea what that 10-dollar word meant but nodded like I did.

Consulted a dictionary later. Damn. My boss was brilliant indeed.

Coach Chapman and his staff loved the idea, too. So, I wrote the story.

There in the pages of the paper was a photo of Chapman and me glaring at each other, face-to-face. He's quoted as saying his team "will win at least five games, probably even seven".

Of course, my reply was that his prognostication was ridiculous, mainly "because you're talking about little ol' Belvidere boys, kids who always quit when the going gets tough. You'll be lucky to win four games."

Oh, yeah? says he.

Yeah! says I.

Wanna bet? says he.

Hell yeah! says I.

So, if — somehow — Chapman's team was fortunate enough to win more than four games, I'd let the players and coaches cut my shoulder-length locks. They could choose the time and place.

And just like *that*, the community and Chapman's ridiculed-in-print players went ballistic. Instantly, parents inundated me with nasty letters. Folks stopped me on the street, asking, "Why are you making fun of our team, our children?" Worse yet, they hounded me incessantly at the local watering holes. I'd merely smile and say, "Well, we'll let the season results do the talking."

Belvidere won the season opener against Rockford West, 26-0. For the first time ever. In Saturday's game story I praised the team yet followed with an ass-kicking column the following Monday. Kept sticking the needle to them, saying, "Calm down, folks. It's only *one* victory. My hair is still intact."

The Bucs clobbered Rockford Harlem the following week, 31-8. Again, praising the team in the Saturday game story. Inserting the goading needle in Monday's column: "Okay, two wins — whoop-de-dooo!"

Week 3: Bucs blister Jefferson, 55-0. Newspaper circulation skyrockets. I'm cheering on the inside, yet writing: "Did you ever wake up and think that everything that's happening is a bad dream? Looked in the mirror this morning, my hair's still there. Thank you, Lord, I'm smiling."

Seems I can't go anywhere without being chastised. Can't even enjoy a beer anymore without being heckled. Worse yet, an anonymous local cartoonist, who identified himself as "The Phantom", starts taking me to task, dropping off derogatory illustrations about me in the dead of night at the *BDR's* front door.

Worse: *BDR* publishes them!

Week 4: Bucs win a nail-bitter against Freeport, 27-26. Yikes, I publicly admit in Monday's column that I'm getting nervous. "It's gut-check time, folks, but I fear not because we're talking about Belvidere kids. Can you spell *Wimps*?"

Subscription boss is buying me beers. "Keep it up, Smitty," he says. "Business is booming."

Doomsday approaches — Friday night, October 20 — and it seems as if every downtown merchant has a sign in its window praising "Buc Pride". And, of course, reminding me time is running out on my long locks.

Dawns the big day, and Belvidere edges the Rockford East E-Rabs, 10-7, on the strength of a 20-yard, fourth-quarter field goal by Rich Rahorn. At 5-0, the Bucs are in sole possession of first place in the Big Nine Conference. Again, for the first time…ever. I wax poetic in the next day's game story, praising the team to high heaven.

I eat crow in Monday's column, saying, "I obviously misjudged this team's intestinal fortitude."

But nothing I write can postpone the inevitable. Coach Chapman calls me at the office Tuesday afternoon, saying the school's principal, Jim McMahon, has everything worked out. The scalping will take place Thursday evening as part of the homecoming festivities at Funderburg Stadium.

"And please let the public know they're all invited," he says, laughing.

My bylined story dominated the *BDR's* front page the following day, accompanied by photos taken by my cohort in crime, Bill Hetland: "First Scalp The E-Rabs, Then John Smith" and "Cut Smitty's Hair".

The headline said it all:

Bucs Scalp John Smith Thursday.

I ate more crow in the story, saying: "Belvidere's boys have finally grown a

pair, becoming men overnight…
learning how to take no prisoners."

Also let the community know the
trimming would follow the annual
homecoming parade, prior to the
bonfire. The parade, which would begin
downtown at 5 p.m., would end up at
the high school parking lot, several
blocks away.

Concluded the story: "It's a sad day
for me but a happy day for the Bucs. At
least there's some salvation. Yes, at least
I'll know how Gen. Custer felt at the
Little Big Horn."

Thursday dawned. The community
was revved to fever pitch…so was its
football team, all of whom had spent the
night before sharpening scissors.

As the homecoming parade made its
way through downtown en route to the
stadium, a police cruiser pulled up to
the *BDR* as scripted. Officer Bill McGill,
known as the local narc, stepped out

and asked, "Where did you get the shirt?" which had State Prison stamped on the back. Told him a friend of mine, Gene Rhode, had let me borrow it.

"It's appropriate," McGill said, then pointed to the prison number 45873 emblazoned on the front, and added, "That's the number of hairs that's gonna be chopped off your head."

I cringed, wondering if Officer Friendly knew something I was unaware of, that maybe the team and coaches planned on doing the deed with an axe or butcher knife.

McGill, who remembered me from my teenage days in his town and all the trouble I'd caused him, grabbed handcuffs from his belt, smiled the smile of a man who thoroughly enjoys his work, and slapped them on my wrists. The CLICK was the loudest sound I'd heard in an awfully long time.

"Tell you what," he said, again with a mischievous grin. "Gives me a lot of satisfaction. Been a long time coming."

He placed me in the cruiser's back seat, got behind the wheel, hit the siren, and lit the top of his cruiser. In short order, we entered the stadium through the maintenance gate, cruising along the track that circled the playing field, this to the raucous cheers and jeers from a standing-room-only crowd — including my wife, June, and our daughters, two-year-old Julie and four-month-old Jill. There had to be more than 1200 watching, easily the biggest crowd of the year.

Officer McGill, his hand securely grasping my left forearm, perp-walked me across the field. Clustered near a microphone in the middle of the field were the entire Bucs team, coaches, cheerleaders, and BHS principal Jim McMahon. The noise was deafening.

Everyone screaming for blood…I mean, hair. The BHS band happily played a dirge, tooting and drumming a death march.

Greg Pollock, a defensive stud who delighted in destroying opposing running backs, took the microphone and said: "The football team and our coaches voted this afternoon after practice that we would wait until after we win the Big Nine Conference to cut John Smith's hair."

Handing the microphone to me, I responded, "Thank you. My wife will appreciate this. She's my beautician, and she had tears in her eyes this morning but now she'll be happy. After all, I only have one head of hair to give for my football team, so I'll gladly wait until y'all clinch that Big Nine title."

The noise from the crowd was deafening, decibels rising a thousand-fold. Then deadly silence followed by ominous footsteps behind me. Before I could react, cold steel was applied to my head. Yikes, I'd been conned. Double-crossed. The vultures had circled and pounced. The team bum-rushed me like fire ants to molasses. Each player and coach took turns methodically clipping off a handful of hair. Everyone laughing maniacally, even me. Then it happened. What the crowd, hell, the whole town, was waiting for. Each assailant lifted his cherished fistful to the thunderous cheers of one and all.

Yes, I humbly accepted my fate. Before you could say Yul Brynner, I was bald.

Well, almost bald. Not barber buzz-cut-tight-to-the-skin bald. No. They left me raggedy-assed, as if they'd used an ice-cream scoop, gouging out long swaths of hair here, leaving a tiny chunk there.

Upon viewing the scene of the crime, my wife joyously cried.

Yet, somewhere out there in the land of big-time sportswriting, I knew my mentor, George Plimpton, he who introduced me to "participatory journalism", was smiling and saying, "Well done, John, well done."

Friendly persuasion?

Doug Chapman, Belvidere High School football coach, and BDR Sports Edit
John Smith have a difference of opinion on the length of one's hair. Both hav
agreed to let the outcome of the '72 Bucco season decide whether or not Smi
gets his locks sheered. Smith says 'no sweat' while Chapman is already buyi
scissors. — BDR Photo — Hetland

Doug:
"Our team is not wimpy."

Jedwin:
"Oh, yeah?
Shall I recommend
a way for them to
grow a pair?"

It doesn't pay to write bad checks with your mouth. Just ask BDR Sports Editor John Smith. Assistant football coach Rich Hetland is shown putting the finishing touches on Smith's haircut. The BHS football team did the most damage though, both to Smith's hair and five Big Nine opponents. — RDR Photo - Hetland

Rich Hetland:
"Payback's a bitch,
ain't it?"

Jedwin:
"Just take a little off
the side, please sir."

All hail
The Ponytail!
The sheep has
been shorn.

POSTSCRIPT

The following night, in a steady downpour, Belvidere High's homecoming was dampened as the home team lost to Rockford Guilford, 21-14. I'd like to think the Bucs were simply beaten by a better group of street fighters, that they had not left all their brilliance lying on the field the night before with the remnants of my clipped long locks.

Not to be denied, though, the mighty Bucs won their next three games, finishing an 8-1 season — the best in 25 desperate long years — as co-champions (with Guilford) of the 1972 Big Nine Conference.

And in all the seasons that followed — standing tall, unflinching and victorious — were a football power, forever to be feared.

POST-POSTSCRIPT

In the 47 years since receiving my just rewards that was the scalping from the magnificent 1972 Belvidere Bucs football squad, my returning to the community had always been a painful requiem for several reasons. So painful, in fact, that when I moved my family to Florida in 1973, I had planned not to ever return.

As pointed out earlier, I never bought into the concept of having what normal folks call a "hometown". Arriving in Belvidere during my senior year in 1963 was our family's seventh city in 11 years. I attended five junior high and two high schools in that time. I was always the new kid and always leaving old buddies behind.

Forever the odd man out.

Always an outsider looking in.

Also, the most painful event I've ever experienced, saying goodbye to my younger brother and best friend, Jeff, who in 1968 was killed in action in Vietnam, happened in Belvidere. My mother, June Elizabeth, forever grieved by me and forever grieving her dead son, was felled 10 years after Jeff's death, and buried beside him, where else but in Belvidere.

Add my brutal alcoholism, reckless temper, and obsession with finding the Viet Cong commander responsible for Jeff's death and killing him (told in my third critically-acclaimed book, the memoir *Our Brother's Keeper*) — well, you can see, bottom line, Belvidere held too many bad memories.

In the late summer of 2019, however, my wife, a Belvidere native who returned home to friends and family on a yearly basis without me, set up a book signing at the community's newly refurbished museum. Having contacted schoolmates from her Class of 1965 to tell them about it, they heavily marketed the event. I reluctantly agreed to return to what I considered "just another port of call". But I went back for June who, I now believe, was God's instrument in helping this old man learn a lesson he much needed.

Can't adequately explain how wrong I'd been all those years. The signing was packed with friends and well-wishers, almost all of whom greeted me with hugs and handshakes and "I almost didn't recognize you, Smitty — especially now that you've got a full head of hair." Big laughs all around. Felt great. Couldn't turn around without someone saying how much they missed me, and how they'd always bragged about my writing, and the success I'd attained.

Dear God. What was going on? He was teaching me, that's what.

Georgia is always on my mind and good things happened here, too. But today, when someone asks where *home* is, my heart is instantly overwhelmed with good memories and I declare with no hesitation: "Belvidere, Illinois".

Thomas Wolfe got it wrong in his 1940 novel *You Can't Go Home Again* because I did go home again.

And when I returned to wonderful Belvidere after so long keeping them at arm's distance, I discovered that I was remembered. More importantly, though, and thoroughly stunned about, was how much the community *loved* me. So, there I was, remembered and loved and experiencing it, I think, for the first time. I spent most of that first day with old friends holding in tears. God knows how hard June and others tried through the years to tell me — show me — that I was loved and valued by them, but I just didn't get it.

I think songwriters Kenny Loggins and Michael McDonald sum it up best in a song they released in 1978 (just six years after that Bucs winning season) called *What a Fool Believes*. Two short lines say —

> *What a fool believes he sees,*
> *No wise man has the power*
> *to reason away.*

What a fool I'd been...but God loves fools, too.

Miss Atlanta travels everywhere with her pet skunk, Napoleon, a docile creature who makes his mobile home in a small, but comfortable, carrying case. BDR photo — Smith

Rita likes to make money

She's no different than the average American

By JOHN SMITH
BDR Staff Writer

What do you tell your wife when you're about to interview a world famous stripper?

If you're like this writer, apprehensive, unsure and feeling uncomfortable about the whole thing . . .you don't tell her anything.

That's what happened earlier this week when the chance to interview Rita Atlanta came across the desk.

Rita, who is currently performing at Frank Gay's Marquee, is in what could be called the "unclothing business." That goes to say she's a stripper, a take-it-off young lady and a crowd pleaser.

especially in the case of Rita Atlanta. Instead of finding a hooting, unintelligent 'loose woman', you find, instead, a woman who likes to think of herself as a self-styled journalist, who speaks four different languages, who, in all reality, is a lady and not a 'tramp.'

Miss Atlanta started her show business career at the age of five as she traveled with her actor-father throughout the movie sets of Vienna, Austria.

'I never really liked the movie circuit because it just was too strenuous,' said Rita as her manager John Winfield Baloe, an ex-prize fighter, poured us an ex-prize fighter, poured us coffee. "You'd have to get up at 5 a.m. to catch the trolley to the different movie sets . . .it just was too much. After that I took music lessons in Vienna

"how could a girl ever do anything like that?" She said she couldn't and continued as a clothed belly-dancer through Europe and the Middle East

It was in the Middle East, in Tripoli, that she met and eventually married a U.S. Air Force colonel . . she was 18 and in 1959 they entered the United States. It was here that her career moved from belly-dancing to stripping.

"American law said that you had to be 21 to perform in nightclubs as a belly-dancer and I was told that in order to continue my career as a dancer I would or could perform as a stripper," she added. "I did and that's how this all started."

And now she is making $1,000 per week, even a $50,000 home near Boston, Mass., travels

1973

Champagne, anyone?

It was my going-away present to the newspaper and Ms. Rita's going-away present to me.

A Friday afternoon. May 1973. My last week at Illinois' *Belvidere Daily Republican*. The *BDR* was the first port of call in my 36-year-long newspaper journey. I'd just accepted an offer to work in Cocoa, Florida, covering the region's 20-some-odd high school athletic teams for *Cocoa TODAY*. I've always been a gypsy at heart; or, as my critics often said, I was leaving town just ahead of the posse. Whatever the reason, greener pastures always appealed to me.

The *BDR* news staff consisted of six of us; our circulation, at best, was 6000. *TODAY's* staff was mammoth in comparison. The sports department alone consisted of a baker's dozen writers and editors with circulation nearing 60,000. To be sure, it was a giant step upward.

Bottom line, my career was on the upswing. Granted, I'd done my part, attacking the job with passion, often working seven days a week at the expense of a growing family — June and I now had two beautiful daughters to nurture, Julie and year-old Jill. But, due to the patience of associate publisher Pat Mattison and the guidance of managing editor Bill Hetland, I'd been molded into a competent reporter and writer. I was counting my blessings.

All of which brings us to my final hurrah at the *BDR* in May 1973. We'd just put the afternoon's edition to bed when, amid a loud declaration from the front desk receptionist that "you can't just walk in there", in strolled this beautiful, provocatively dressed brunette. From my point of view, she was a knockout. Sashaying through the newsroom, hips swinging erotically, smiling sensually, and gently cuddling a furry critter in the cradle of her left arm.

Believe me, you could have heard a pin drop. Hetland was gawping at her. Dorothy Coombes, our society page editor, was shocked into startled silence. As for me, my eyes were bleeding.

Okay, I'm exaggerating at bit. My eyes were like that cartoon wolf — bulging out a foot or two, its hormones off and running.

Before Hetland finally regained his ability to speak, the lady in question introduced herself as Rita Atlanta, then demurely asked, "Would anyone like to pet my pussy?"

I kid you not. Hetland started laughing. And then I remembered the ad that was running in the bottom right-hand corner of page 5, announcing that the World-Renowned Queen of Burlesque, Rita Atlanta, would be appearing outside the city limits at the notorious Marquee Lounge that night and Saturday evening —

With her pet skunk!

Which was the furry critter she cuddled in her arm that afternoon. Indeed, the provocative damsel had a way with words. Hmmmm! What a story this would be; that was part of my thinking. The other part...well, I was a typical testosterone-filled 27-year-old; all sorts of erotic possibilities were flashing through my head and...let's leave it at that.

One thing led to another, and my boss wondered if Ms. Rita was worth a story. Quickly realizing Hetland was a frickin' genius and would go far in the newspaper game, I agreed to do the interview with nary a fuss. I drove out of town to the Marquee nightclub, whereupon I was introduced to Rita's manager. Got a cramp in my neck looking up at the dude, who I thought I recognized as a former boxing champion in Great Britain. Six-foot-forever, chest as massive as a rodeo bull's, Popeye-like biceps, and hands the size of uncured hams.

The creature nodded, expressionless, as if descended from one of those Easter Island stone statues, and hovered just to the left of Rita Atlanta. Fantasies evaporated and a rookie's interview was conducted along the lines of a PG-rated movie. The burlesque queen steered me through her career. Innocently, amid the room's perfect lighting. Didn't bother to ask her age; could tell by the makeup and exhaustion within her eyes that she'd traveled many miles.

Nonetheless, she was stunning. And surprisingly pleasant to converse with.

Somewhere during the interview, she invited me to attend that evening's routine. "Part of my performance is done in a large champagne glass," she coyly intoned. On cue, Mr. Brahma Bull handed me a free ticket, which included a complimentary beer.

Drumroll, please.

So, there we were, four score and seven or eight males — some of whom had actually brought their wives or dates — sitting around tables coyly surrounding the biggest champagne glass I'd ever seen. Me? I'm sitting at the bar, trying not to be noticed as I worked on my free beer. I mean, Belvidere is a small town, where everyone knew everyone else and...well, my conscience was working on me. Also had a splitting headache; too many concussions, crushing right hooks to the head, and whatnot. Was anticipating what would happen when my wife of seven years would see Ms. Rita's feature story in the next day's edition.

Whoops, forgot to mention that I'd failed to tell my bride what, precisely, I was up to. "Working on a story" is all I'd said. Up to that point, she was a trusting beauty who worked during the day and mothered our two young daughters in the evening.

So, with my conscience synchronized to the migraine, and visions of Crockett and Bowie during the waning moments at the Alamo, the lights dimmed. Background music softy played. Then a spotlight zeroed in on that humongous champagne glass half-filled with water, from which rose large bubbles. The other half of the glass was provocatively filled with Ms. Rita.

What? Whoa! In the nude?

Couldn't tell for sure because of all them damn bubbles floating up and about — and the way our burlesque queen had her legs strategically tucked beneath her, and her right hand holding the big sponge across her chest.

"And now, ladies and gentlemen," the announcer intoned, "Rita Atlanta will now proceed to take her bubble bath."

Deafening applause, plus a few whistles. Had my beer bottle raised to my lips when the man with the mic said, "But first, the lovely Rita needs assistance. We need someone to assist washing her back."

And just like that, the spotlight nailed me at the bar. Thought I heard someone shout "Cong in the wire." Then the announcer said, "John Smith, please step to the stage."

Felt like someone had nailed me in the solar plexus. Beer spilled down my chin. *You've gotta be shittin' me?*

I'd like to say I boldly stepped forward. Fearlessly grabbed hold of the sponge Ms. Rita demurely offered, popping bubbles left and right, and scrubbing away in voyeuristic delight.

But I would by lying because I was terrified...of June.

Caught red-handed in a sensual game of five-card stud where the lady across the table had called my bluff. Me red-faced while holding a pair of deuces, The Queen of Burlesque flashin' a pair of...well, you get the picture.

Ms. Rita giggled.

My hands shook.

Ms. Rita giggled some more.

And my legs grew weak as I hesitantly, and most gently for fear of breaking something, ran the sponge over her back. Were this a movie, at this point June would have burst through the lounge's door, pistol in hand, and...you know the rest.

Thankfully, June never heard what Ms. Rita said next.

My reverie burst when, in a coy voice, but loud enough for everyone to hear, she said: "Oh, honey. You missed a spot."

Big laughs from the audience and my face was aflame.

Was told the crowd loved the performance. Proving once again that, despite what those ol' hormones of ours are saying, what we think we'll do and what we *actually do* are light years apart.

POSTSCRIPT

Yes, my lovely bride was pissed the next day. She hadn't seen the paper yet, but friends and family burned up the phones, laughing at my expense, wondering how June felt about all the notoriety. Especially the promo picture of Ms. Rita covered up by bubbles in that big champagne glass which accompanied the story.

Funny how life works out. June's "I can't believe you did that" in Belvidere echoed all the way to those distant Florida shores a few months later. We were cutting across Florida to the Gulf Coast to visit my aunt. So, there we were. Windows down, enjoying the balmy air. Our children snuggled in the arms of Aunt Dorothy back in Bradenton. June had calmed down from the Ms. Rita story by then, blaming the entire episode on my episodic drinking.

We were on a gravel road outside of Sarasota heading to the dog track when we passed a billboard:

Rita Atlanta
Appearing Tonight Only!

Made a fast U-turn. Pulled into the tavern's parking lot. Threw open my door and told my bride I'd be right back. Returned a few minutes later and asked, "Would you like to see the woman who made a fool of me?"

Indeed, she would.

There were no fireworks, however. Instead, Rita, all smiles and truly a lady of virtuous poise and propriety, shared with June the beauty secrets that kept her looking so young — the various creams and lotions and advised that, whenever possible, never to venture out into the sun.

And June? She simply smiled in return and shared her love of Jesus; even prayed for the Queen of Burlesque. Best part was seeing the startled look on the face of Rita's wild bull of a manager as June also prayed for him.

Big-eyed and red in the face, he was. His reaction reminded me of mine months earlier while peering intensely at the near-nude lady in the bubbly champagne glass when Ms. Rita coyly said, "Oh, honey, you missed a spot."

Spring Training: Part 1

1974

Hammerin' Hank Goes Deep

It was March 2, 1974, and I was en route to West Palm Beach's Municipal Stadium, spring training home of the Atlanta Braves. Nervous butterflies ricocheted around my stomach like free-flowing ammo in a firefight. This was my make-or-break moment: Prove to my boss, *Cocoa TODAY* sports editor Ray Holliman, that I could produce well-written stories in a Major League setting. Which is why he'd sent me to interview "Hammerin' Hank", Hank Aaron as otherwise known.

I was pumped.

Talk about big-time pressure. Of course, mine was nothing compared to what Aaron was facing. So, there I was, driving south down I-95 with memories of long-long-ago yesterdays about my brother and me spending summers at the "friendly confines" of Wrigley Field. Hanging over concrete-and-brick railings near third base, we hoped to snag an autograph or have a chat with our baseball heroes as our Cubbies warmed up by taking infield.

The Braves franchise moved around a bit until finally finding a home in Atlanta. From Boston to Milwaukee in 1953, then relocated to Atlanta in 1966. Those ol' Milwaukee teams always left me demoralized because they were constantly beating my forlorn Cubs. Unmercifully. Knocking 'em down. Driving a wooden stake through their collective heart.

With a firm grip on that wooden stake were future Hall of Famers Eddie Mathews, Joe Torre, and Warren Spahn. And always wielding the proverbial hammer was Hank Aaron, the immortal mortal — the greatest Brave of 'em all.

Except for that little awestruck kid trapped within me, time had marched on. And it marched for "Hammerin' Hank", too.

For the 20-year veteran of the Braves, life had abruptly changed for him in the '73 season when he'd hit 40 home runs. He now had a 713 lifetime total, leaving him one short of Babe Ruth's four-decade-long record of 714. That made the 40-year-old Aaron the media's primary target. Trapped in the stardom of the moment, his every move was examined under a microscope.

Constantly surrounded by cameras and reporters and hounded by the specter of possibly, maybe, daring to, surpass The Bambino, the game's hallowed Sultan of Swat, Aaron was not liking reporters at this time.

Within the first four days of spring training in 1974, Braves management figured Aaron had reached the breaking point. He'd been bombarded enough. Which didn't bode well for this rookie reporter, for upon my arrival at Municipal Stadium I was informed that Aaron was off-limits to the media. Quarantined from all reporters for reasons unspecified.

Still undaunted, I'd given it the old college try as he walked off the field and into the dugout, asking for a few minutes of his time. Without looking at me, Aaron brushed past and said coldly, "Not now, not now. I've got to change my shirt."

Well, that was a bummer. Actually, my internal language was a bit more colorful. I'm sure you can guess what I actually thought. Obviously, Aaron did not understand my job pressures either. Ended up interviewing the Niekro brothers, Phil and Joe, both knuckleball pitchers. It was a decent story, but it was not Hank Aaron — *the* big-time story of the year.

Later that early evening, I pulled into the parking lot of a somewhat seedy bar. Can't remember the name of the establishment, other than it had dim lighting and was filled with smoke. At the time, my kind of place. Entered, fired up a cigarette and took a seat at the bar. Paying no mind to the clientele. Wallowing in disappointment. Ordered a beer and drained half of it when, from a few chairs to my left, came a voice: "Saw you out there at the stadium this morning. Did you get what you were looking for?"

Turned and was greeted by Braves manager Eddie Mathews. He smiled and pointed to the "Smiling Braves" logo on the big press badge pinned to my left breast. The Braves PR department identified credentialed members of the media as a security measure. "Our way of assuring everyone that you weren't a kook," Mathews said, chuckling.

I was going to say lots of folks out there might disagree with that assessment of me. But I held in my smartass and smiled instead. "Yeah, disappointed I couldn't interview Aaron," I said.

Mathews eased the pain a bit by buying me another beer. Thanked him, raising the bottle in a toast to "Hank breaking The Babe's record". A few more rounds purchased back and forth and next thing you know, we're chatting it up.

"How did you end up as a sportswriter?" Mathews asked.

Now my smartass had a few beers and let fly. "They called off the war in Vietnam."

Soon, I'm telling Mathews a story from the 1964 season. About my future wife's surprise going-away present the day before I took the big bird to San Diego's Marine Corps Recruit Depot to report to Dante's Second Circle of Hell, otherwise known as boot camp.

"Sunday afternoon. June seventh. County Stadium against my Cubbies," I said. "We've got prime sixth-row seats midway between home plate and first base. 'Course, I'm on edge because I'd never seen my Cubs beat you guys. Seems as if you and Hank owned Wrigley Field, hittin' homers at will. And I pretty much was sick and tired of [pitchers Warren] Spahn and [Lew] Burdette makin' fools of us, mowin' us down."

Mathews' eyes mellowed, his grin enormous. "Yes, sir, what a great day it was. Bright sunshine, plenty of cold beer. And the bratwurst. Best I've ever had. Better yet, Ernie Banks hits a two-run homer in the fourth inning, Billy Williams goes deep with a two-run dinger in the sixth, and even Andre Rodgers hit a solo shot in the ninth."

Couldn't help myself and poured salt on an old wound. "'Course, ol' Hank rips a two-run rocket to left in the fifth inning. But damned if we didn't finally win, 5-2. That was great. Twenty-four hours later, I'm almost wetting my pants as this Neanderthal DI is screamin' in my face."

Took a breath and a gulp of beer, knowing Mathews was enjoying the hell out of the reminiscence. We order another round, after which he clarifies what's going on with his superstar. Mathews said there had been lots of racial taunts, hateful letters, and phone calls as Aaron crept closer to Ruth's home run mark. Even more of it now.

Mathews said, "I'm a little leery of the kooks — the weirdos — who might come out of the crowd someday to do something [bad] to Hank. You know, all kinds of shit like that."

I cringed. Told him that's why the good Lord invented the Colt .45, to protect good folks like Hank from idiots. Eddie gave that some thought, nodded his head a bit, then asked where I was headed next.

Jokingly I responded, "Going back home. A beaten man."

He grinned. "Show up at the ballpark tomorrow morning around 10. I'll make sure Hank talks with you."

And there they were the next morning, sitting in the dugout. Mathews looking worse for wear from the night before. Aaron's hands wrapped around a bat. Eddie nodded as he rose and stepped away, allowing me to sit down. I thanked Hank for taking the time to speak with me, then asked about the racial threats, Mathews' mention of weirdos and kooks possibly coming out of the stands; was he fearful —

"I don't want to talk about that," Aaron said icily. Yet, his head darted from side to side, as if looking for someone to walk in on him. "That was last year. That's all forgotten now."

I decided to swing for the fences, journalistically speaking.

"All right, but what about the team's announcement that you won't be playing in the season-opening series in Cincinnati? That you'll sit out those three games in hopes of hitting numbers 714 and 715 before the home fans in Atlanta. I know a lot of writers have criticized you and the Braves for this."

"To hell with the writers," Aaron snapped. "The writers didn't say a damned thing about Stan Musial when he sat out a game in order to get his 3000th hit before the home fans. And the writers didn't say anything about Roberto Clemente when he did the same thing."

Aaron paused, stared toward center field. His hands still drawn tightly around the bat. He looked at me, eye-to-eye, and said coldly, "That story broke during the winter, and I guess the writers didn't have anything else to write about. I don't have to prove anything to the writers. This is my life and I'll do whatever the Braves and I think is best. I've got an obligation to our fans. *They're* the ones I want to please."

Without another word, he stood, grabbed his helmet, and headed to the batting cage.

I had my story. What journalists call "a nationwide breaking story".

As I would find out 29 months later — having moved on as the fledgling sports editor of the *Racine Journal Times* and Aaron now an aging member of the Milwaukee Brewers — Hammerin' Hank had never forgiven me for the intrusion.

That verbal *mano a mano* reunion appears later.

POSTSCRIPT

Commissioner Bowie Kuhn pressured the Braves into playing Aaron in the season-opening series in Cincinnati, ordering him to play in two of the three games. On Opening Day, April 4, with Kuhn in attendance, Hammerin' Hank homered off Jack Billingham to tie Ruth's record. He sat out the next game, then went hitless in game three.

The Braves' home opener was Monday night, April 8, against the Dodgers with a capacity crowd of 53,775 at Atlanta-Fulton County Stadium — minus Kuhn, who said he had more pressing business in Cleveland. Aaron drew a walk in the second inning.

In the fourth, however, with Darrell Evans on first via an error, Aaron hit the second pitch delivered to him from Los Angeles pitcher Al Downing over the left-field fence into the Braves' bullpen, where it was caught by relief pitcher Tom House.

With that 715th homer, Henry Aaron humbly accepted the crown as the game's greatest home run hitter of all time. Long live the King!

Spring Training: Part 2

1974

The (Bleepin') Earl of Baltimore

Received a bunch of kudos for the Aaron interview of two weeks past, enhancing my status among Florida's top sportswriters. Which, to my way of thinking, meant I dare not let down my guard, keeping my eye on the prize of being the best among the best, having to constantly prove myself — sorta like one of them Wild West gunslingers.

Awoke on March 18 to face a new test, this one awaiting me at Pompano Beach Municipal Stadium, spring training home of the hapless Texas Rangers. First in the hearts of

Arlington's faithful. Dead last in the American League West.

The Texas Rangers were an afterthought. A team of oddities managed by an oddball, to quote my boss, Ray Holliman. In fact, he had quite a bit to say about those woebegone boys of summer from Texas.

"No one's ever made the mistake of using *outstanding baseball* and *Texas Rangers* in the same sentence," he said.

Further educating this rookie reporter, he said they even managed to turn the collective stomachs of Congress. That's right. The Texas Rangers were the Washington Senators.

He said, "The Senators were so horrendous and repulsive they were run out of town on a rail and renamed and relocated" to the environs of Arlington, squeezed between Fort Worth and Dallas. Enough said.

Today's mission, should I successfully pull it off on behalf of Gannett's ever-expanding newspaper chain, was to interview the Baltimore Orioles' Brooks Robinson, Mr. Baseball among the game's third basemen, and the Orioles' all-time hits leader; MVP of the 1970 World Series; MVP of the 1966 All-Star Game; the American League's MVP in 1964; and winner of the Rawlings Gold Glove Award as the game's best defensive third baseman the past fourteen seasons.

The Arkansas man's brilliance with both bat and glove was unquestioned, especially in the eyes of my boss, an Alabaman by birth. "So, lemme see what y'all can do with this-un'," he said, knowing that I knew he was a Robinson junkie, both of them bona fide Sons of the South.

Left unsaid yet definitely implied was this: Y'all hit a homer with Aaron, so I'm expectin' at least a double with ol' Brooks. Was I nervous? You betcha.

Never could stomach losing; was bound and determined to pull off this interview. Nonetheless, couldn't shake that image of W.C. Fields dismissing me with his standard shtick:

"Go away, *kiiiid*, ya bother *meeee*."

Which just might, indeed, be the case with this assignment. After all, I'd been forewarned by Holliman: "Problem with spring training is the regulars aren't always available; it's sort of hit and miss."

Leaving that piece of pessimism dangling in front of me for a few seconds, he added with a tongue-firmly-planted-in-cheek grin, "Who knows, ya jus' might haffta improvise. Now, if'n it was me and Brooks was a no-show, I'd say ya could always try wrasslin' with Weaver."

Gee-zus!

To say the irascible Earl of Baltimore — the volatile Earl Weaver — was a difficult interview is to wallow in understatement, mainly because if you caught him at the wrong time, every third or fourth word had to be eliminated. The King of the F-Bombs, that he was. Can't say he possessed a gutter mouth. Hell, his was the entire sewer system. The Orioles manager didn't just swear like a sailor — he swore like the Navy's entire Third Fleet.

Over the past six seasons, the 44-year-old Weaver had made a career of being ejected from baseball games. An ornery ol' cuss, he'd made quarreling into an art form. Forever arguing umpires' decisions. Getting banished for kicking dirt or even pitching dirt on them. But mostly for arguing spasmodically with "them blind sumbitches" and questioning the legitimacy of their birth.

Shuddering, I silently prayed that Brooks would be there, then asked Holliman, "What about the Rangers?"

"Being's yer a Cubs fan," he said, "ya might get lucky and catch (Fergie) Jenkins. Other than that…ah, I don't know, mebbe ya —" At this point, Holliman had trouble keeping from gagging on his RC Cola. Tried a second time; failed. Third time was the charm and he continued. "Over in the other dugout is Billy Martin and…well, one thing's fer certain — you ain't gonna be bored. Not with Weaver and Billy Martin in the same ballpark."

Quickly shelving all the bad vibes coming my way, I thought about something positive — successfully getting that Brooks Robinson interview, plus something readable from the Rangers' side of the ballfield.

Arrived at the stadium, too early to grab a hot dog and a few beers. Had time on my hands. No players warming up out on the field yet. Knowing anything from the home-team Rangers' point of view was secondary, but that attaining a sterling interview from Baltimore's Robinson was the brass ring I'd been assigned to grab onto, I nervously stepped toward what I assumed to be the visiting Orioles' clubhouse door.

Ready or not, Brooks, here I come. Hesitantly knocked, my nerves on edge.

The door sharply swung open. And I was stunned into petrification, for staring back at me were the shark-like eyes of Baltimore manager Earl Weaver.

"What the (bleep), kid — you lost?" Weaver glared, like he was ready to gnaw off the head of a snake, while the rest of his coaching staff chuckled.

"Ah, sorry, Coach."

Weaver's eyes turned demonic. "Well, excuse us all to hell," he growled, eying my press credentials and the ever-ready pen and notebook in hand. "It's not like we've got anything (bleepin') better to do, so why don't you step on in here and take a (bleepin') seat," he motioned to the empty metal chair next to him. "C'mon, just set your ass down and, you know, we'll like shoot the (bleepin') shit."

By now, his coaching staff was busting a gut, laughing their asses off. I froze like an old deer caught in the headlights. Felt like the village idiot for choosing the wrong door. Finally found my tongue, said, "Ah, sorry, Coach. I didn't —"

Weaver shook his head in despair. Grabbed his cap and comically beat it against the concrete floor. Took a deep breath, composed himself then, in a civil tone, said, "Let me guess. Yer new at this, right?"

Before I could answer, he softened his tone even further and said, "Let me enlighten you. Football and basketball have coaches. Baseball? These guys sittin' here with me, they're (bleepin') *coaches*. Me, I'm the (bleepin') *manager*. Think you can remember that?"

Apologies tripped all over my tongue. Admitted I was, indeed, a stupid neophyte; all this big-league stuff was new to me. And, damn, I sure was sorry for inciting his anger…

Then I swung for the fences again and said, "…even though my boss warned me you sorta get a kick out of making us squirm. Scaring the hell out of sportswriters."

Weaver liked that admission. And from that point on, the interview went without a hitch. Got everything I needed. Sarcastic grin in place, he even thanked me for stopping by.

Breathed a sigh of relief once I stepped out of the Oriole manager's office, softly closing the door, thankful to still be in one piece. Having been chastised greatly, yes. Not to mention being humiliated for my choice of doors to knock on. But nonetheless, having stood my ground despite a panicked voice from deep inside screaming for me to run like hell.

Could feel the ghost from yesteryear, that of my old Marine Corps drill instructor, finally rewarding me with a smile, telling me the "smoking lamp" was lit and, while I was at it, saying I might as well reward myself with a hot dog and a couple of beers.

Ooh-rah!

Spring Training: Part 3

1974

My Heroes Have Always Been...

Appetite sated, I went in search of Brooks Robinson. Although Earl Weaver had provided a few usable quotes about his star third baseman, those would ring hollow unless I was able to corral the future Hall of Famer himself. As it was, my luck held true as I re-entered the Pompano Beach Municipal Stadium playing field through the press gate and immediately ran into Brooks Robinson on the infield grass.

Once again, that little kid inside me stammered, "Ah, excuse me, Mr. Robinson —"

He smiled, cutting me short with a comical look. "Call me Brooks."

In no time at all, I was smiling ear-to-ear as the game's greatest third baseman ever proved to be the perfect gentleman, politely answering questions for a good 20 or so minutes with me excitedly jotting down his comments and floating on air. At the conclusion, I wasn't embarrassed in the slightest when that little kid in me profusely thanked him and shook his hand.

Felt ten-foot tall as I turned into the sun, looking for another interview. The search was interrupted by a penetrating voice to my left: "Pretty decent guy, ain't he, kid?"

Turned toward the Rangers' side, where mustachioed manager Billy Martin sat amid the shadows of the home-team dugout, waving me on over. My knees grow weak. Instantly awestruck. Took a deep breath, swallowed my nervousness and, with just a little bit of trepidation, nodded and reverentially took a seat.

"Looked like you were having a good time out there with Robinson," said Martin.

Although overwhelmed by the moment, I managed to say, "Even more so, now."

All sorts of emotions raced through me, mainly because I'd spent most of my youth idolizing only two baseball players, Ernie Banks and Billy Martin. Banks — the Chicago Cubs shortstop; always smiling, never uttering a discouraging word. Battlin' Billy Martin — the brash, toxic, foul-mouthed second baseman of the New York Yankees.

"Might sound funny coming from a sportswriter," I stammered, "but you've always been one of my heroes."

Martin didn't miss a beat. "Maybe that's because you haven't spent a lot of time around me, until now." He laughed at that, then I introduced myself, told him this was my first go-round with spring training and how my boss was gonna be pleased that I'd managed to snare the Orioles' star player. What I didn't share was the racing fear, how my mind was at warp speed, scrambling for questions that wouldn't elicit a right hook.

Martin shifted his eyes to Robinson who was fielding ground balls at third, then studied the newbie at his left, sizing me up. Nodded and hit me with a disarming, charismatic smile. "Didn't think I recognized you, kid. But it's obvious you enjoy your work."

Paused, then said, "Yeah, always a good thing to keep the boss happy."

Couldn't help but share his laughter about that last statement. Saw the black-and-white photo montage of yesteryear skipping through my mind:

Martin lunging on the infield grass, making the game-saving catch of Jackie Robinson's wind-blown pop-up in Game 7. Saving the 1952 World Series for the Yanks.

Martin celebrating being named MVP of the 1953 World Series after a record-setting 12 hits.

Martin years later with Cincinnati, clobbering Cubs pitcher Jim Brewer after a brush-back pitch.

The newspaper clip files I'd saved about Martin's two prior stints as a manager — both reclamation projects.

The barroom brawl with Minnesota Twins pitcher Dave Boswell in 1969.

Twins owner Cal Griffith describing how having Martin as his manager felt like sitting on a keg of dynamite.

Martin fired after leading the once-woebegone Twins to the AL West title.

Mercurial Martin, hired by Detroit in 1971, flipping over the locker room's food table after a disheartening loss, yet again turning a dreadful team into 1972 AL East champions, then fired in September 1973 for insubordination.

Now here he was, managing the Rangers. He must have been reading my mind because he asked, "Whatcha thinking, kid?"

Couldn't lie to him; my response: "Chaos. Don't get me wrong, I'm not trying to be a smartass. I'm just —"

"Just tryin' to get yourself a headline; I understand. So, don't be afraid to ask."

Once again, he'd taken me by surprise. So, I complied: "You once said that fighting brings a team together; that it's the little things, not big home run innings, that win ballgames. Stealing signs, stealing bases, the hit-and-run…"

Mentally thumbed through the background information I'd accrued. Found what I was looking for: "Bunting, the suicide squeeze, the double steal, and stealing home. You know, old school baseball — Billy Ball, that's how some writers define you."

Paused, then added, "And some others think you're a lunatic."

Martin's laughter echoed throughout the otherwise empty dugout. His eyes darted to left field, where his outfielders were shagging flyballs. Then graciously wondered aloud, "So, you think maybe we should talk about how this raggedy bunch of players of mine intends to do this season?"

Yes, please. I asked about the previous two seasons, the Rangers losing a combined 205 games, finishing dead last both times. Asked about the pothole-filled managerial road that brought him to Arlington, Texas — fired by the Minnesota Twins in October 1968, despite guiding the team to a division title; fired in September 1973 by the Detroit Tigers, then hired six days later by the Rangers.

"I'm a two-time loser, but I know how to win," was his response.

All in all, Martin was forthright, surprisingly easygoing. Downright charming, in fact. Providing a solid rundown on what most pundits thought was an uninspiring team. Didn't dodge questions, said he'd traded for former All-Star pitcher Fergie Jenkins from the Cubs, believing Jenkins still had something left in his right arm. Offered no apologies for his temper, his past quarrels with players and general managers or team owners. Never did broach the subject of his drinking, though. Hell, I had my own problems. So, I let that sleeping dog lie.

Martin's greatest strength? He damn well knew baseball.

His biggest fault? He damn well hated losing.

Laid my pen and notebook aside, content as any rookie could be, knowing I was batting three-for-three in the Big Leagues. Counted my blessings, thankful that nothing I'd asked of him had provoked a punch in return. Then stuck out a hand and thanked the man who made loving baseball a lifelong pastime.

Martin returned the gesture, then shifted his gaze to the outfield, where five or six of his players were warming up, fielding fly balls. Amid this group was Jeff Burroughs, pantomiming dizzily, turning in tight little circles as a flyball came floating down and fell harmlessly at his feet.

"Burroughs!" Martin screamed, ripping his ballcap off as he stormed out of the dugout, throwing his cap toward the infield grass, and waving angrily for Burroughs to come hither. Which Burroughs did, without hesitation, stepping lively toward a thoroughly irate Martin.

All these years later, I close my eyes as what happened next plays out in slow motion. The look on Burroughs' face is sheer terror, even though at age 23 he's 6-1 and a chiseled 200 pounds. He slows his pace, stopping five or six steps from Martin, twice Burroughs' age, a wiry 5-10, 160 pounds.

Martin yells something undecipherable, but nary a punch is thrown. Burroughs hangs his head, hands passively at his side. Martin throws an arm over the kid's shoulder and from all I could see, he's speaking civilly as player and mentor step slowly in tandem down the left field line.

Shouldn't have been surprised.

But I was.

POSTSCRIPT

Spent the next four hours sitting in the best seat in the house, up high and directly behind home plate on press row, not so much worried about what transpired during a meaningless exhibition game, instead typing away on the '74 prognosis story of those no-longer-hapless Texas Rangers.

Led off with a calm and collected Billy Martin speaking from his team's dugout, saying he felt confident his team would have a winning season; certainly, no longer hapless enough to lose 100-some-odd games like each of the previous two seasons. Yes, there appeared to be hope indeed for the Arlington faithful. Way I wrote it, Martin was optimistic his Rangers would learn to hate losing as much as he did. Rise from the ashes, so to speak, becoming winners after being perennial losers, dare I say, in the blink of a right-hand uppercut.

Was about halfway through the story when a hand came to rest on my right shoulder. Turned around to see Red Smith, the legendary sports columnist of *The New York Times*. He politely asked if he could see what I'd written on the first page.

I eagerly complied.

Can't tell you how long he stood there, reading and then re-reading what I'd composed, before saying, "You've got a great future ahead of you, son."

There are no words to describe how I felt at that moment.

POST-POSTSCRIPT

Over the course of the next six months, those once-unlovable Rangers surprised the baseball world, finishing second in the AL West with an 84-76 record, behind the eventual World

Series champion Oakland A's. Rangers first baseman Mike Hargrove was named AL Rookie of the Year, while batting .323; Fergie Jenkins was named the Comeback Player of the Year, having won 25 games; and Jeff Burroughs, who never again clowned around in the outfield, earned AL MVP honors, while batting .301 with 118 runs batted in.

Billy Martin could do no wrong that year, guiding the franchise to its first-ever winning season, proving once again that he "damn well knew baseball", being named the American League's Manager of the Year.

He was fired in August the following year for ordering the public address announcer to play John Denver's *Thank God I'm a Country Boy* during the seventh-inning stretch instead of the traditional *Take Me Out to the Ballgame*, which the team owner demanded.

1974

The Unkindest Cut of All

Watched all 108 candidates practice that first day as they meandered first through calisthenics before breaking off to join their individual coaching specialists — running backs, offensive linemen, wide receivers, quarterbacks, and a whole passel of defensive experts.

"So, what do you think?" asked Jacksonville Sharks head coach Bud Asher, as he sidled up to me at the team's training facilities at Stetson University in DeLand, Florida, in May.

Wanted to say the ensemble looked like a handful of officious dudes with whistles trying to herd cats. Instead, I merely nodded and maintained my silence, not having the heart to burst Asher's bubble.

After all, enough of my brethren in the world of sports had spent a lot of time poking fun at this new professional football concept — the World Football League. It was composed of 11 nationwide franchises, complete with a plethora of National Football League rejects, fair-to-middling college stars, and countless hundreds of borderline wannabes from all walks of life.

After less than two seasons, this concept would prove to be a financial failure. But until the wooden stake was hammered into the collective heart of this greatly alleged and exceedingly hyped fiasco, the role I played was in being assigned by *Cocoa TODAY* as the Sharks beat writer. I was excited about it. Reporting daily from the team's training facilities, plus covering its games, kept me busy — and out of the bars. Of greater importance was not being stuck at the office behind a desk editing copy from other writers.

Had a few misgivings, though, especially when it came to the Sharks' organizational chart. Team owner Fran Monaco was a 5-foot-4 DeLand millionaire with a penchant for custom-made bright-green checked suits and silk ties, plus a Napoleonic leadership style. When the Florida Tourist Board voiced its outrage over Monaco naming his franchise the Sharks, saying the name and team logo would discourage tourists from visiting Florida beaches, Monaco stood his ground.

His wife, Douglas, second-in-command, stalked the sidelines with her miniature poodle, parading back and forth in front of the team bench, which not only thoroughly pissed off the coaching staff but also lent a comical air to the machismo sport.

And then there was head coach Bud Asher, whose only professional football experience was scouting for the NFL Oakland Raiders and San Diego Chargers. The rest of his wide-ranging resume included coaching the semi-pro Daytona Beach Thunderbirds, municipal judge, owner of several area hotels and a geriatric hospital, and, most recently, the former coach of Florida's New Smyrna Beach High School's football team. Fight on, you Barracudas!

Not that team-owner Monaco viewed Asher's lack of big-time experience as a detriment. In fact, during the team's initial press conference, Monaco boasted that Asher would not only be the greatest of all WFL coaches but "It is my feeling he'll even be better than (the late Green Bay

Packers coach Vince) Lombardi and (Miami Dolphins coach Don) Shula."

Asher's tenure would end after six games into the team's 20-game season, fired after a dismal 2-4 start amid public outrage and a team-wide insurrection. "He treated us all like we were little high school kids, not men," said one unhappy player.

These uncertainties would be addressed in the days and weeks ahead, but for now I was in search of a whiz-bang, attention-grabbing feature story in which to enhance my growing reputation — and ambition of moving up the ranks to cover a *real* professional football team, notably the Miami Dolphins.

With that in mind, I attacked the present job with vigor. The initial glut of aspirants was trimmed to a workable 80 or so players after the first few days of practices. After that, I scanned the roster in search of potential prospects.

One name in particular jumped out: Oddie Lawrence (pronounced O-dee), a mammoth defensive lineman at 6-foot-4 and 255 pounds. Hadn't laid eyes on him yet. Knew nothing about his football pedigree. His first name was odd; that is what piqued my interest.

Also was curious about the odd notation designating which college football program Oddie was affiliated with. Others on the roster had played for big-time schools like Georgia, Auburn, Florida State, etc. Beside Oddie's name it stated NC. Figured the Sharks PR guy got lazy and instead of typing in the University of North Carolina, shortened it to NC.

So, approaching defensive line coach Russ Faulkinberry, I inquired about Oddie. Was told in typical coach-speak: "In pro ball, football on this level, it's just a matter of how your desire is locked up. Here, everybody has ability. You get the cream of the high school crop plus the cream of the college level." Faulkinberry paused, seemed embarrassed to continue. "Oddie tries very hard. He's one of the most sincere and dedicated kids I've ever coached."

That was an odd thing for him to say. Which piqued my curiosity further. What did he mean? The assistant shuffled his feet, paused again, awkwardly looking for the right words. "I mean this when I say Oddie's the type of person anyone would like to have as his son."

Good grief! Had Oddie been diagnosed with an incurable disease? Faulkinberry shook his head, bit his lower lip, and finally said the big dude's prospects of surviving the final roster cut weren't all that promising.

"But then again…"

That statement was left hanging in the heat and humidity of the practice field. For the time being, Oddie would be a formidable obstacle to block and run through.

In parting, Faulkinberry said, "Wish I had something more positive to tell you. Problem is, it's tough trying to compete on a professional level, near impossible without experience. See, Oddie, he's greatly handicapped because he didn't play college football."

Whoa, figure the odds on that? So that's what NC stood for: No college.

For the time being, Oddie Lawrence would remain on the roster for the express purpose of being used as a blocking dummy. Expendable cannon fodder. Of optimal use right up until the final roster cut. And then it was anybody's guess what his fate would be — more than likely, slim and none.

Nonetheless, my gut told me to tag along with this no-college lad. Or maybe it was Someone Higher had me stick around? Whichever, if Oddie Lawrence was willing, I'd be his shadow for the next couple of weeks compiling a major feature story, giving readers a progression diary-like presentation of one young man's pursuit of living the dream — becoming a professional football player.

First step was getting the big dude's approval, which is never an easy task and usually involves a mix of excuses — everything from "I've got too damn much on my plate right now" to "I just don't trust any of you (bleepin') reporters."

Oddie, however, threw me a curve. Upon approaching him after that afternoon's practice, he seemed flat-out dumbfounded that I was paying attention to him.

Oddie Lawrence:

"My boys gonna
be real tickled
to read about
their daddy."

"Coach tol' me you be a-wantin' to do some sorta story? That true?" Oddie said, his words soft-spoken and chosen with extreme care, as if he couldn't understand why the hell I was interested in him. Not that he was upset about the prospect; far from it.

"My boys gonna be real tickled to read about their daddy," he said, a magnanimous smile spreading across his bearded ebony face; it was almost enough to make you overlook the thick, indented scar running across his forehead.

And his dark eyes were momentarily joyful — kindly eyes that in the days ahead would cloud with darkness and confusion; eyes that appeared to have witnessed more horrid times than most folks at age 25 would ever experience. Which I soon was to discover was true.

For now, though, those eyes of his were sorta dancing with excitement as we sat in the wooden bleachers beside the practice field, his massive girth providing a bit of shade for me. He peeled off the sodden practice jersey and then his shoulder pads, revealing an even worse-for-wear and greatly soaked T-shirt.

Before I could ask about the ghastly, inch-thick scar running up the length of his left arm, he said, and not without a touch of wariness, "I'm not Notre Dame or Oklahoma or any of those other big schools like the rest of the guys out there."

He paused, his eyes downcast, and obviously embarrassed as he added, "I'm...uh, coach tol' you I've got no college, right?"

I nodded. "Doesn't matter, bro. I'm likin' what I see." He smiled. I paused, then asked, "About those scars, where'd you get 'em?"

Just like that, Oddie's demeanor changed as he somberly explained there were no college scholarships waiting for him when he graduated from Mathew W. Gilbert High in Jacksonville. And because there were five sons and seven daughters in Jacob and Marie Lawrence's family, there was no money to send Oddie to college.

"So, I joined up with the Marines in '66, ended up bein' a demolitions expert," he said. "Next stop, Vietnam. Deactivating enemy landmines and booby traps. Really hot over there, almost as hot as out here today." That brought out a big smile again as he chuckled and said, "Well, not really."

Gave the former Lance Corporal and Purple Heart recipient a Semper Fi shout-out and fist-bump, which solidified our mutual trust.

Voice almost a whisper, he said, "We was workin' on a bridge near Khe Sanh when the Cong opened up on us with mortars. A buddy of mine got killed in the initial attack and I really started to wonder what the hell I was doin' there."

He paused and raised his hands to his face, then rose, shook his head, and jammed his massive fists into the air. "And boom! There was a flash — that's all I remember."

Oddie left a lot of skin and blood, not to mention a portion of his soul, in that Southeast Asia hellhole. And now here he was, seven years later battling for respect on a much tamer battlefield — making amends for yesterday's missteps in pursuit of his version of the American Dream.

In the days that followed, I came to know Oddie as well as I knew my own brothers and sisters. Which is disconcerting, mainly because such knowledge and familiarity comes with the good and the bad. Lots of good times, watching him at practice busting heads and having the time of his life. And too much of the bad, witnessing him missing assignments and being pushed around, both of which prompted reprimands from coaches.

And then we'd retire to his room, going over the day's events. Much aware of his shortcomings, self-evaluating the pros and cons, he refused to make excuses.

"It's very difficult for me here because I have so much to learn...to catch up on," he said, the words coming slow and choppy. "I've had to learn the most basic things myself...with no college ball...well, guess I just don't know all the basics."

Those basics he did grasp came courtesy of "a passel of hard work and a whole lotta prayer". On one hand, he played semi-pro ball for three years in Georgia with the Douglas Tornadoes;

and then shouldered additional responsibility two years ago by marrying his wife Anna and, in the process, gaining three stepsons: Karl, 12; Reginald, 11; and eight-year-old Martin.

"When the Sharks had a tryout in Jacksonville," said Oddie, "I told everyone I'd bring home a contract. They all smiled at me and then we all prayed about it. Yessir, my wife and family are a-hopin' and a-prayin' for me. They always be a-prayin' for me and they are very, very beautiful."

Leading up to that initial tryout, Oddie worked fulltime as a Jacksonville longshoreman and part-time on a shrimp boat. No frills, just grueling toil for solid pay. Giving up that financial security was not easy.

Then again, neither was abandoning his dreams.

"I saved enough money to keep the family okay before I came here," he said. "My wife is still workin' at a day job — she cleans other people's homes."

With that, he said he'd better get back to work. "Lotta things to catch up on," he said, pulling out the three-ring binder in which the Sharks' defensive schemes were outlined. Thanked me for taking the time to chat, said we could talk some more the next day.

He grinned and added, "That is, if'n you think I still be worth it."

Over the course of the next week, the excruciating hot sun and two-a-day practices melded into grueling monotony, broken only by Oddie's ongoing struggle to make the grade. His unique way of expressing himself kept my mind off the heat, too.

"Some of the guys on the other side of the ball are really something else," Oddie said. "Ain't nothin' easy 'bout battlin' up front against Florida. And

Georgia Tech can wear a soul out, tryin' to bring him down."

He paused, shaking his head in wonder. "Been gettin' some help from ol' Ike, though. He's been helpin' me out a lot, takin' time to give me some pointers. A real nice guy, that he sure is."

Had to call time-out to pop some aspirin, onaccounta Oddie was giving me a headache. Never been good at conversing in code, and for the past ten minutes or so the story I'd been working on was rapidly running off the rails. With the exception of Ike, who I assumed to be NFL veteran defensive end Ike Lassiter, I had no idea who or what the big guy was talking about.

Oddie looked dumbfounded when I asked who the hell was Florida?

Why, he's the first-team offensive guard, he said, which led me to grab the team roster and scan down the list until

I got to Larry Gagner, the 6-3, 240-pound All-America guard from the University of Florida.

"Sorry. Have trouble tryin' to remember everyone's name; sorta makes my own head hurt," Oddie apologized, poking fun at my sudden need for aspirin. "Names, no. But I do knows what college they played for. All of 'em, except Ike."

Told him Lassiter played at St. Augustine's College in Raleigh, North Carolina, in the early '60s. Oddie replied, "Never heard of that one."

Promised not to share that with Ike.

Nonetheless, it seemed like at some point in our weeks-long conversations, Oddie's fixation on having not played college football was an ever-present albatross dangling round his neck. The Georgia Tech dude he'd referenced was quarterback Eddie McAshan. As for Lassiter, at age 34 the oldest player on the roster, once upon a time he was the starting defensive end for the Oakland Raiders in 1968's Super Bowl II.

When I asked about Lassiter's help, Oddie reached for his playbook and tapped both sides of his head with his gnarled hands. "I didn't know defenses had these many plays. And when I looked at 'em all, it was confusing. Have trouble memorizin' 'em all. You have to be thinkin' all the time and sometimes I forget the plays and it make me mad."

And then he started thumping his head harder. "Get so mad that...don't matter, none. See, I can't afford to make no mistakes, not if I want to make this team. There be no room for my mistakes, not none. But Ike's been there a-helpin' me; helpin' me lots."

His frustration was growing, so when he asked if we could take a little break, I reached for my cigarettes and stood in the open doorway as he picked up the telephone and rotary-dialed to connect to the outside world.

As soon as he said, "Hello, Mama, this be Oddie…" I politely waved good-bye and said I'd see him tomorrow afternoon.

Got an admission to make. As professional journalists, we're supposed to remain impartial. Just gather the facts, jot down the respective comments from both sides of the issue, and biblically let the dead bury the dead.

Spend enough time with a given individual, though, hearing him dumping his heart and soul at your feet, impartiality gets in the way of one's heart. And — truth! — I've pretty much always worn my heart on my sleeve.

The more I played fly-on-the-wall to Oddie Lawrence's *Don Quixote* quest at realizing his dream, the more I wanted to kick in the door of the Sharks' brass and beseech them to sign this brother to a long-term contract.

What pushed me to the edge of his emotional abyss were a few chats in the coming days with Oddie's family:

During one of our after-practice sessions, Oddie was agonizing about his inability to grasp the team's defensive schemes as quickly as the other players. Then, as if chastising himself for again delving into the negative, he spoke of his mother, Marie.

"My mamma raised 12 children and she is a remarkable woman. She say, 'Oddie, have patience, son; keep on a-hopin' and a-wishin' and always be a-keepin' God on your side. By holdin' God close to you, you can overcome anything.'"

And while Oddie was at it, Marie said, "And don't forget to thank God for you still bein' alive, hear?"

When I telephoned 59-year-old mama Marie, she said Oddie "has worked hard all his life for this one particular day. He's always wanted to be a professional football player and it's something from that little-bitty boy that's still in him.

"You see, my boy's never had no platter handed to him. He's worked hard for everything. This is something he's always wanted and I'm just a-prayin' he makes it because he wants it so, so bad."

Marie then handed the phone to her husband, Jacob, who echoed her.

"His whole life, I'll tell you that's all Oddie's wanted to do — it's always been professional football," said Jacob, 64. "Tell you what, before he left home for this camp, I'm wantin' to know if'n he's makin' the good decision. So, I asks him, I say 'Oddie, is this *really* what you wants to do?' And he tells me, 'That's *all* I wants to do, daddy.'"

One man's dream.

That's what all of this came down to.

Oddie's obsession to overcome his lack of a higher football education — laying his passions and love of country on the line, just like he did seven years earlier in Vietnam — hoping and praying good intentions will be enough to carry the day.

"You know, when I's back home I'd get up in the mornin' and run, then go to work, and then come home and be a-liftin' weights just to get ready so I could make this team," Oddie mused during the final days of training camp. Absent was the tension, the frustration, that usually engulfed him.

Now, instead of worrying, the big dude was grinning, even as his eyes filled with tears.

"I be at home and my wife and the boys would sit with me at night and rub my muscles with rubbing alcohol. And my boys — oh, my boys are really so proud of their daddy — they keep saying 'My daddy's a professional football player'. But I keep sayin', 'Sons, you hope I be a professional football player.' You know, a man's gotta keep on a-hopin'."

But all hope died on Wednesday morning, June 26, 1974, when Oddie Lawrence was summoned to the coach's office and handed a bus ticket that would carry him back to Jacksonville.

It is difficult to cut someone with Oddie's size and innate ability to play football. A man his size and with his ability makes marvelous cannon fodder for the troops.

Oddie would have accepted any role in professional football, even as cannon fodder during practice.

As it was, the Sharks' coaching staff told him maybe he was good enough to work on a shrimp boat, or on the docks in Jacksonville, but not good enough to play football on a professional level.

How do you reconcile a man who has just been told he is not good enough to do what he wants to do when he's doing what he's always dreamed of?

"It's not the end of the world," Oddie told me on that fateful morning, his head cupped in his hands, his eyes welling with tears. "I'll be a-tryin' again next year. But…"

His voice broke as the tears fell steadily. He reached out to thank me for taking the time to hear his story, then took a deep breath and said, "I'm no quitter. But the hardest thing is gonna be tellin' my boys…"

And for Oddie Lawrence, that was the unkindest cut of all — but not the end of Oddie's story.

My story on Oddie ran on Sunday, June 30, 1974. Quite a boost to my ego, it was. Even so, I felt terrible for him — his rejection, not being good enough to make the grade, being splashed from coast to coast. Hell, the story even brought tears to my eyes.

Carried that sadness with me all the way to the Sharks' season-opening game on Thursday evening, July 11, 1974, at Jacksonville's Gator Bowl against the New York Stars. With almost 60,000 fans in attendance, the noise was deafening. Despite the clamor, I heard my name shouted as I walked the sidelines during pre-game drills.

I turned and…

Good grief, there was Oddie running toward me, screaming — at me! My first thought was I was a dead man for humiliating him in print. But I thought, didn't he go home? So what's he doing here? But his screaming was that of jubilation. He ran me down and picked me up with those massive arms of his, embraced me and swung me round and round, shouting he'd just been signed by the Sharks.

Whoa! What? Once Oddie's story was published, and then went national, the Sharks' front office was bombarded with calls and letters from far and wide. Everyone demanded the team find a place for the former Marine.

The Sharks did not ignore the wisdom of the crowd and found a place for him: Oddie was signed to the practice squad, where his abilities were most needed. Of course, the league only lasted two years, but for those two years, Oddie's Dad, Mama, brothers, sisters, nieces, nephews, wife, and stepsons saw his dream — and their dream for him — come true.

And you know what? That's not a bad thing to have happen.

POSTSCRIPT

Oddie Lawrence died of natural causes on Wednesday, November 14, 2018, at age 70, and is buried at Jacksonville National Cemetery; Section 10, Site 1141. He was preceded in death by his parents, Jacob and Marie Lawrence; his son, Karl Jeffery; sisters, Dr. Rudyne Sherfield, Molly Newsome, Ella Mae Lawrence, Gloria Stephens, and Beverly Dawson; brothers, Jacob Lawrence Jr. and Leon Lawrence.

1974

"Don't Let the Door Hit You in the Ass."

Nineteen-seventy-four saw my journalistic career skyrocket. I'd been hired by Florida's *Cocoa TODAY* in June the year before as its high school beat writer; I covered the circulation area's 20-some-odd high school athletic teams: football, basketball, baseball, etc.

The beauty of working in the Sunshine State was its competitiveness: a dozen major newspapers and three premier athletic factories (Florida, Florida State, and Miami), all recruiting from the state's plethora of nationwide top-ranked high school athletes.

In short, a sportswriter's dream come true — work your butt off, hone your craft to the razor's edge, and you easily could and would rise among the ranks. The way I attacked the job was honed in my youth: I might not be the brightest bulb in the house, but I sure as hell would outwork you.

Turned out, my high school beat lasted less than six months. Come January 1974, the state's biggest story was Florida State's search for a new football coach; Larry Jones had resigned two weeks earlier following an abysmal 0-11 season. Sports departments across the state scrambled to beat each other, speculating who might take over the Seminoles' struggling program.

Among those head coaches allegedly under consideration were Vanderbilt's Steve Sloan, Kansas State's Vince Gibson, Kent State's Don James, and Western Illinois' Darrell Mudra.

Except for Mudra, the others had served as FSU assistant coaches.

Having arrived at work Tuesday afternoon (January 8), after reporting on high school basketball the night before, I telephoned my cousin, Tom Carper, a star running back for the Western Illinois Leathernecks. Asked him about the rumors of Coach Mudra being in the running for the FSU job. Was jolted when he said everyone on the team knew Mudra was going to get the job.

"It's a done deal," he said.

Did Tom have Mudra's unlisted home number? Why, yes, yes indeed he did. And when I dialed it, one of Mudra's sons answered. I identified myself, asking if I could please speak with his father. "I'm sorry, sir," came the reply, "but he's out of town right now. We don't expect him home until after the weekend."

My mind went to working a mile-a-minute. "I also have a number for him in Tallahassee. Might I be able to reach him there?"

The kid's reply: "Yes, sir."

With that information from the boy, plus a conversation with FSU alumnus Walter Revell — state Transportation Secretary and spokesman for the Seminoles' six-man committee appointed to name Larry Jones' successor — I was on my way to a sure-fire scoop. Revell enthusiastically supplied me with this gem:

"You know Darrell's called 'The doctor of sick programs', don't you?"

I didn't, but I did now — which is how I broke the story in the next day's edition that Darrell Mudra "was expected to be named later this week as head coach at Florida State University".

Overnight, I was promoted to the college football beat. Mudra was the first of many stories I would break nationally. Equally important was the 15-dollar weekly raise.

Anyway, with my journalistic stock continually on the rise, *Cocoa TODAY* sports editor Ray Holliman informed me 10 months later that I'd be accompanying him to Miami early Sunday morning to help cover the Dolphins' game against the Atlanta Falcons. Ray would write his column and game story; I would be responsible for writing sidebars about the Falcons.

Piece of cake, I told the boss. Yes, I was cocky as only a rising star among the Fourth Estate could be.

Have typewriter, will travel!

Over pregame beers in the Orange Bowl press box on that momentous November 3, I dropped the line I would use throughout my newspapering career: "Give me a weapon and enough ammo, designate the target, and I guarantee I'll destroy it overnight."

Ray liked my bravado. But in this instance, he passed on a word of warning: "Step softly around Coach Van Brocklin. If it were me, I'd be a bit leery of 'im."

I gave him a sidelong glance. "The Dutchman? Hell, he's always been one of my favorites. Wore No. 11 with the Eagles when he led 'em to the NFL title in 1960. Same number I wore in high school. I idolized him. Man's tough as nails."

Ray grimaced. "Yeah, and the flip side is he can be as mean as a snake, especially when he's losing. Word to the wise, tread easy when you get in the Falcons' locker room. Man's volatile; doesn't take much to get under his skin. And you can be...you know, you can be a bit irritating sometimes."

Couldn't help but smirk.

"I'm serious," Ray continued with his warning. "Van Brocklin's easily pissed off. And the Falcons are..." Ray paused, looking for the right word.

I beat him to it. "Lower than whale shit," I said, sharing the laughter.

Game time came and went. True to form, the Falcons were pathetic. Miami beat the bejabbers out if them, winning 42-7, handing Atlanta its third straight loss, its sixth in eight games.

I scurried into the bowels of the Orange Bowl, following the Atlanta media into a compact room no bigger than a walk-in closet. Didn't bother to count, but it was wall-to-wall sportswriters. Gathered in a tight semicircle around a fraught Van Brocklin barking short replies to a couple of mundane questions.

Yep, the man's on edge; keep your cool. Think of something intelligent to ask.

Another mundane question.

More growling from the Dutchman.

Holliman's warning echoing in my head: *Don't be an irritant.*

With that, I screwed up my courage, having come up with a viable question. "Coach," I said, "you've had a lot of difficulty in your rushing attack the past —"

Dutch's eyes glared at me, then he uncoiled like a viper. "What? What'd you say?"

"Ah, your offense has had a tough time on the ground. Was wondering —"

"Wondering? Why don't you just 'wonder' your way outta here."

I looked at his hands, both bunched into big-knuckled fists. Oops! The man is 6-1, 210 pounds. And I'm Barney Fife with a reporter's notebook. I looked around the room, the walls of which seemed to be closing in on little ol' me.

The sportswriters maintained their silence, all eyes on the accused. Gawkers at the scene of an impending accident.

Glanced back to Van Brocklin, whose eyes were those of a shark. He snarled, "Well?"

Well, hell, Coach. I was tongue-tied. Not believing what I'd stepped into. Was gonna inspect the bottom of my shoes but thought better of it. Wondered what my mentor, Hunter S. Thompson, would say if he were here. Smiled, knew he'd scream *Dutch is about to go bat-shit!*

Silence.

An extraordinary amount of silence.

Then finally, "Who the hell do you think you are, asking a stupid-ass question like that?" Van Brocklin yapped in a high-pitched voice. Not exactly frothing at the mouth, but spittle was a-flyin' in my direction.

Huh, know the man's only 48, but his mind's slipping; he's repeating himself.

Who the hell am I? Gee-zus!

I resisted the urge to double-check the name printed in bold letters on the official press pass hanging around my neck.

"Stupid-ass questions, all of 'em. So, why don't you get the hell out of here?"

Questions, plural? Hell, I'd only asked one. Nope, he'd only let me ask half of it. But don't push your luck. Wait 'im out, the orderlies will be in soon to sedate him. Patience, m'lad.

His arms were raised to his chest, moving back and forth. Not like he was ready to throw a punch. But his blood was boiling, no doubt about it. The volcano was about to erupt.

"Go on, get the hell outta here, boy."

Boy? I smiled, attempting to dampen the fuse. Which only pissed him off some more.

"Go on, get — and don't let the door hit you in the ass on the way out. Hear me? Don't let the door hit you in *the ass!*" Which prompted laughter from my audacious peers.

So, I would leave. Subdued and greatly humbled, the image of my childhood hero thoroughly shattered. Yet, still capable of flashing that leprechaun's smile and a smartassed wink of an eye. Which further enraged Van Brocklin.

"Yeah, get the hell outta here and" — spittle a-flyin' everywhere now, and me knowing it was time to bid this little intervention adieu.

The sporting gang moved aside, offering me an exit. I slowly stepped to the door, pulled it open, then stepped through.

Stopping midway, though.

Making sure it hit me on the ass on the way out.

Back in the press box, I was working on a sidebar about the Brothers Malone

— Art, a running back for the Falcons; Benny, a running back for the Dolphins — when Ray Holliman approached and said, "Damnedest thing. Heard that Van Brocklin almost got into a fight with one of the writers. You didn't by chance see it, did you?"

Took a swig of beer. "Yep, I'm the guilty party, Your Honor."

"You're shittin' me. What'd you do to piss 'im off?"

"Asked him about his team's shitty running game. He went ballistic."

Holliman burst into laughter. "Think it's worth writing about?"

"Not my call. I mean, I'm still new at this — besides, no punches were thrown," I said. "No harm, no foul. It's not like this is something new for him, right?"

Holliman nodded. "Okay, I'll just add a note at the end of my column."

The next day, at the Falcons' weekly press conference, an Atlanta reporter who'd been in the room with me the day before asked Van Brocklin if he was still a fighter, as he had insisted several weeks earlier, considering the season was slowly going down the toilet.

The Dutchman glared at the writer and immediately challenged him to a fight. The coach then extended the invitation to about a dozen other writers, broadcasters, and eager photographers in attendance.

Norm Van Brocklin was fired the next day.

I'd like to think the door hit him on the ass on his way out.

1975

The Story I Never Wanted to Write

I never got a chance to know Tim Dobson from a subjective standpoint.

What I saw of his high school gymnastics proficiency was condensed into a handful of seconds, as he propelled his wiry frame on the high bar, spinning up and over, moving ever so gracefully, spinning at speed up and over the bar again, before attempting his finale — dismounting with a half-turn pirouette, intending to land feet-first onto a cushioned mat.

One horrific split-second later...

"It all happened so quick." Tim's coach, Gerald Hodgin, would relive what happened next. "Tim was going into the final part of his routine, and I turned to the next gymnast and told him to get ready. And then..." Hodgin paused to calm his tearful emotions. "And then I saw Timmy coming off the bar in a semi-crouch..."

At this point, all the coach could do was mentally scream — *No-No-No!* — for Tim's dismount was greatly flawed. Tragically flawed, in fact, as the 17-year-old junior miscalculated his dismount, falling face-first onto the mat, breaking his neck.

The accident was at approximately 9 p.m. on Tuesday, May 6, 1975, in the Merritt Island (Fla.) High School gymnasium. I was there, covering the performance because my bosses felt I needed a lesson in humility. And they were right. Seemed like everything I'd touched over the past two years had turned to gold, and accompanying the glory were excesses — too much nightlife, too many beers and high times; too much immaturity on my part. What better way to humble this lad, bursting that inflated ego by taking away the professional writing beats and making him endure.

That evening's assignment was expected to be punishment and indeed it was...

...but not what the brass anticipated.

All these years later, I close my eyes and lay hands over my ears and can still see Tim Dodson's head hitting the mat, twisting at an atypical angle less than 10 feet in front of me. And despite the muffled ears, I still believe I hear the distinct CLICK — which told me the rest of the dominoes were about to fall.

It would be three days before I returned to the sanity of the newsroom

— staying beside the Dodson family most of the time, sleeping in my car when necessary — and wrote the story I never, not in my wildest imagination, ever wanted to write. A story that began this way:

> "For all practical purposes, 17-year-old Tim Dodson is dead."

Yes, it was a brutal way to begin. Yet factual. The result of an accumulation of agonizing hours spent with the Dodson family, friends, and the family pastor, all of whom attempted to make sense of tragedy and failed.

I knew how they felt when, seven years earlier, a Marine Corps officer and a staff sergeant knocked on our door to inform Mother and me that Jeffrey had been killed in action in Vietnam.

For some unfathomable reason I would become quite expert at putting tragedy into words that outsiders could understand. No matter how many times I did, however, it never got easier. Something inside dies with every story.

After telephoning the *Cocoa TODAY* sports desk, informing them about the accident and saying I'd provide additional information later, I sped the 25 miles to Melbourne's Brevard Hospital where Tim Dodson was listed in critical condition; comatose, sustained only by a life-support machine.

Doctors put Tim's recovery chances at a mere five percent.

Although no one wanted to admit it openly, Tim's mother, Sue, anguished a few hours after the accident that it would take a miracle to bring her son back.

Later still, an unidentified Merritt Island High School official would tell me: "Now would be a great time for Jesus Christ to pick up lots of converts because only a miracle can save Timmy now."

There was lots of coffee and even more prayers among those who kept hopeful vigil throughout the night and following day. Yet Tim showed no improvement; he remained unconscious, paralyzed from the neck down, still on life support.

Between offering up prayers, the Rev. Jimmy Jackson of Merritt Island Baptist Church shared observations with me that at first sounded somewhat beneficial, yet when seen in print would appear jarring: "Tim was doing something he liked to do....You can't wear diapers all your life. Why, kids get hurt walking down hallways at school."

Coach Hodgin nervously paced the halls of Brevard Hospital, unable to wrap his mind around the tragedy.

"You can ask yourself thousands and thousands of time, and it's always the same," the 11-year veteran gymnastics coach said, his hands trembling, his voice wavering. "It's always…" He stopped; his head rolled from side to side, eyes filled with tears. "It's always the same. You just can't explain it."

Wednesday morphed into Thursday. Still no improvement in Tim's condition, so the family adjourned the vigil for a few hours, inviting me to their home. I felt awkward, despite Alvin and his wife, Sue, commending my compassion. Alvin apologized for not speaking with me earlier. "I wanted to, but…" He shook his head, seemingly embarrassed. "I wanted to, but I also didn't want to."

No apology was necessary, I told him. Then briefly shared about my brother's death in 'Nam, the toll it took on our family. "This might sound trite," I said, "but I sorta know what you're going through. I don't want to be a burden. I can leave."

Alvin, a powerfully built individual, a carpenter by trade with silver hair, rejected the offer immediately. "Sue and I were there when it happened. But we couldn't react quick enough, I guess. I just sat there and waited for Timmy to get up. But he didn't."

Sitting across the room, a glassy-eyed Sue, a Merritt Island elementary school teacher, tried to keep her composure, yet failed as Alvin said, "If it hadn't been for Coach Hodgin, Timmy would be dead right now."

Heavy words seeming to echo throughout the Dodsons' living room. An image of Hodgin rushing to Tim's side, noticing he wasn't breathing and immediately applying mouth-to-mouth resuscitation. I simply nodded in agreement to Alvin's stark admission.

Tim's brother Steve, 22 and the oldest of four, had nothing to share except irritation as the phone kept ringing constantly and friends knocked on the front door to console the family.

When his father told me, "We encouraged Timmy to go out for sports. We helped him along, and we'd do it all over again the same way," Steve left without comment and went for a walk.

Stepping outside in need of a cigarette, I was joined by Tim's sister, 19-year-old Robin.

"I went to see Timmy last night," she said, tears welling in her eyes. "I didn't want to…I didn't want to see him like that. There's been no change; my parents haven't told me what the doctors have said."

I didn't have the guts to share what I knew of the impossibility of Tim's condition, so I kept an uneasy silence.

Robin's glassy-eyed gaze was familiar, the thousand-yard stare. She closed her eyes, releasing a deep breath. "There's nothing the doctors can do," she said, absently. "His neck is swollen. He has no feeling below the neck. He's been kept alive by the machine." Her sobs almost drowned out her departing words. "Timmy's chances are rare. No, they are not rare. They are slim."

No, Robin, I thought, Timmy's chances of recovery are hopeless.

With that, I extinguished my cigarette and once again offered my regrets and prayers to the Dodson family, then sped off to the newspaper, grieving heart and soul for another teenage son/brother taken from a loving family way, way too early. And then I painfully and regretfully began typing an epitaph:

"For all practical purposes, 17-year-old Tim Dodson is dead."

POSTSCRIPT

The Dodson family's suffering would continue, as Tim snapped out of his coma a month after the accident, yet remained on life support via respirator, unable to care for himself or speak. His condition never improved.

Thirty-two months following his tragic accident, pneumonia developed in his collapsed right lung, from which he died at age 20. Timmy Dobson was laid to rest on February 3, 1978.

1975

Requiem for a Paperweight

His mouth was moving, but I couldn't hear a thing and he was a blur. I looked out the window. Swamp grass and dead orange trees were a blur, too. And the sunshine — my head hurt like holy hell and the two ice-cold cans of Pabst against my temples weren't helping. I put one between my legs, popped the top of the other, and took a big gulp.

Damn it, even my teeth hurt. Did a quick inventory of all body parts.

Damn it.

Everything hurt.

"No shit, little buddy. I thought you were dead." Riotous laughter from Eric Girard in the driver's seat. "You —"

"What?" I hollered through an incessant buzzing, as if yellow jackets had crawled through my ears.

Eric smiled again and yelled, "You surprised me!"

"Surprised you?" I hollered back, and fired up a cigarette.

"Yeah…you got back up."

Then more laughter. Eric's a natural-born comedian, as well as a boxing aficionado. Which are just two of the many reasons we became fast friends. We were birds of a feather — worked and partied, hard. Which put a strain on my marriage…but more on that later.

Right now, let me start this Hunter S. Thompson-esque tale of "Fear and Loathing" from the beginning.

Before the fight.
"I said *WHAT* at the bar?"

"I said *what* at the bar?"

Eric Girard and I worked at *Cocoa TODAY* and had combined our talents to produce yet another award-winning Sunday sports section. He had made the most of his extraordinary design talents coupled with a damn good Page 1 series by yours truly on visiting Japanese baseball teams. They were participating in spring training with our home-grown Major League counterparts. The main story centered on Sadaharu Oh, 34, Japan's answer to Babe Ruth. Oh had already hit 634 homers and vowed to continue playing until he'd hit 800. [He'd eventually hit his 868th home run during his 22nd and final season in 1980.]

Once the paper was put to bed, we retired to the local watering hole to discuss the world of sports while attempting to quench our insatiable thirsts. One thing led to another and the subject shifted to boxing; in particular, a

fight we'd witnessed at the Orlando
Sports Stadium two weeks earlier:

Mike Quarry, 24, a local Orlando
resident and younger brother of
heavyweight legend Jerry Quarry, won
a ten-round unanimous decision over
Vernon "Sledgehammer" McIntosh.

"Mike Quarry did oooo-*kaaay*,"
Girard wisecracked. "I mean, it was
nothing like his performance against
Bob Foster back in '72, though. Man,
now *that* was an awesome fight."

No kidding. In that bout, Quarry,
then the No. 1-ranked light-
heavyweight, had laid his unblemished
36-0 record on the line in hopes of
stripping Foster of his dual World
Boxing Association and World Boxing
Council titles. Held at the Las Vegas
Convention Center, the fight was brutal,
a vicious, ruthless slugfest in the first
three rounds, Quarry counterpunching,
giving as good as he received.

Girard continued his play-by-play. "Ouch, whatta combination. Foster unloads a right cross, then the left hook in the fourth and down goes Quarry. Lights out! I swear to God, I thought the kid was dead. Fell like a tree being chopped down. Didn't move. Out cold. Laid there for the longest time, arms outstretched. Yeah, everyone thought we'd witnessed someone dying in the ring."

Girard ordered another round of beers. "Yep…sorta disappointed by his showing against McIntosh, though."

More beers. Then that seemingly suicidal dude trapped inside my pea-sized skull blurted: "Gotta agree with ya. Hell, I could've whipped McIntosh."

Thought Girard's neck might've snapped, turning his head that sharp toward me. He slurred, "Yeah? Whutt 'bout Quarry? Think you stay on yer feet with him?"

Nodded, belched, then wisecracked, "Yeah, probably."

Around the world, bragging butts on barstools usually don't have anybody remember what they said.

But not tonight.

Oh, no; not tonight.

The next thing I know, Girard's on the phone with Quarry's people, who were always searching for good publicity for their man-child.

Whoa!

You mean like a three-round exhibition against a wannabe George Plimpton, who'd done the deed sixteen years earlier against Archie Moore with a *Sports Illustrated* story and big pictures to follow?

Hell yeah. Let's get it on.

The match was to be held at the Orlando Sports Stadium on Friday, June 27. Opening bell at two. Good grief, what have I done, thought I upon getting sober and being told by Girard where and when to show up. He was planning the event's page design, headlined by the declaration:

REQUIEM FOR A PAPERWEIGHT!

Yes, he was already having a good laugh at my expense.

I loved boxing and had tried it at the local YMCA when I was a teenager. Was pretty good, too. Learned how to roll under a left hook, bob up to the opponent's left and counter with a right to his head. So maybe, just maybe, doing a first-person story about me stepping into the ring against a top-ranked professional prizefighter will get me more national writing awards plus enhance the family's financial standing.

No harm, no foul.

Piece o' cake.

And talked myself into doing the Quarry fight. But I had forgotten one thing. Drumroll, please. Years ago, I had made the mistake of telling Dad I was gonna quit school and concentrate on boxing. Now, Dad and I seldom saw eye-to-eye. I was a flippant 15-year-old when it came to authority. Said whatever was on my mind. So his response surprised me.

"Well, son, if that's the case, then I'm happy to give you a few pointers."

Mom's response was typical Irish. She asked me to grab her another beer, then quietly cautioned, "Tell 'im you were just shittin' 'im; tell 'im you're sorry." But she knew I was every bit as hardheaded as her. That I was the proverbial lost sheep mentioned in that Bible she seldom opened. Forever the unrepentant youth. She was damn proud of that and knew I was going to the basement.

She smiled.

For those who don't know this, the Marine Corps turned Dad into a killing machine. He heroically survived the best that Tojo's Imperial Japanese soldiers could throw at him in the hellholes of WWII.

Guadalcanal.

Tarawa.

Saipan.

I knew all this. But that was long ago, see. Me being too quick on the trigger, even back then, already considered myself to be one tough nut and he was just an old man. See? He was just a grade-school teacher. Wimpy, you know?

What I didn't know, but Mom did, was that he'd also spent a few weeks after the war as the sparring partner of middleweight champion Tony Zale.

Anyway, Mom accompanied Dad and me to the basement. She laced up our boxing gloves and sat back sporting that beautiful Irish smile of hers, an ever-present beer and cigarette in hand, and watched as Dad beat the bejabbers out of me using my head like most fighters used a speedbag.

Whappity! Whappity! Whap!

Lesson learned.

Forgot all about quitting school. University of Hard Knocks wisdom attained. But not learned quite enough to keep me out of harm's way almost 15 years later.

So, here it is, 1975, and the more I thought about the upcoming exhibition, the more I took a liking to it. The fight was still a couple of months away. Had plenty of time to prepare myself. What was there to lose? After all, George Plimpton, my mentor and the guy who created "participatory journalism", had lost his exhibition fight against Archie Moore and that did nothing but enhance

Plimpton's notoriety. Another book deal was generated. Fame and an enriched wallet were his just for getting whacked.

I was used to getting whacked.

I could do this.

Easy-peazy.

And my training regimen began with gusto. Even though it had been 15 years since I last stepped into the ring, there was no doubt the lapse had done quite a bit to soften my brain as I prepared for the big comeback.

My training schedule was intense. Girard, my brother in crime and now my manager, had me swimming laps in his pool. With every 20 completed came a beer. With every mile run on the beach came another beer. I'd work for an hour on the speedbag and collapse in a lawn chair for two beers and a few cigarettes. Managed to gain a few pounds of flab; digestive system just as fouled up.

Reaction to the upcoming bout was varied:

"You're going against Mike Quarry, the light-heavyweight? You're really going to fight him? With gloves and everything? You're nuts."

Walt Johnson, photographer at *TODAY* who would shoot the fight for posterity.

"He's pretty good, isn't he? Good. Hope he does something to make you grow up."

June Smith, wife of Smartass Participatory Journalist John Smith, on their difficulties of late, having reached the end of her rope, sick and tired of her husband's steadily increasing alcohol consumption and late-into-the-night partying with fellow *TODAY* co-workers.

"No sweat, buddy. We will do alright."

Eric Girard, faithful, ever-confident manager, who had no clue how ironic he was.

"Take it easy on the other Irish lad…but I'll light a candle in church for you — just in case."

Mother of Smartass Participatory Journalist John Smith, also named June Smith; on the night before the fight, by phone, from Belvidere, Illinois.

Didn't sleep much the night before the fight. Tossed and turned. Kept seeing this gigantic fist breaking my cheekbone and rearranging my nose. Two beers didn't help, nor did the pizza. And then came the dawn.

To say I was scared would be an understatement. Never has the Orlando

Sports Stadium seemed so close. Even though I tried to convince it Gainesville was our destination, the car knew exactly where to go. Even more irritating, every radio station I'd zeroed in on was playing that damned Carly Simon song, *You're So Vain*. Yeah, I thought the song was about me.

Knew I was in trouble when my manager gave me a pre-fight pep talk.

"You have to realize, little buddy, that you're not going up against a novice. Three years ago, Quarry fought Bob Foster for the light-heavyweight title. And Foster once fought Ali for the heavyweight title."

That was a pep talk?

Felt some vital organs roiling and thought I was gonna be sick.

"Ah, and there's one other little thing to think about," Girard said, now grinning. "Remember the McIntosh fight back in March? Don't know how many beers you had, but you were heckling Quarry about his inability to put McIntosh away. You kept shouting that he was taking it easy on the dude."

Ladies and gentlemen, please join me in introducing you to a bona fide "Oh, Shit" moment. Yes, not realizing how far my voice carried, I'd carelessly — some may even make the case for doing it unconsciously — made my presence known. Found out quickly enough, because Quarry roughly pushed McIntosh aside, then turned to me and shouted from the ring, "You wanna try your luck in here?"

Huh. Geez. I had forgotten all about that. Thanks for reminding me about it, good buddy.

However, Mike Quarry hadn't forgotten. Oh, yeah. Yeah, yeah…

Yep.

He remembered me alright. As we touched gloves at the center of the ring, awaiting the opening bell, I said, "Say Mike, kinda take it easy on me, okay? Don't kill me."

But Quarry gave me a wicked smile and said, "You're in my house, now."

ROUND ONE

I came out swinging. Unfortunately, so did Quarry. He brushed aside three of my left jabs and then brushed aside my nose with one of his *cr-ack-ack-ack-ling* right-crosses.

When the punch landed, I actually saw that candle Mother lit for me from more than 1500 miles away. Third row, fourth from the left.

Midway through the round, Quarry decides to get cute. He does this shuffle thing. Instinct dictates me to fire a right to the general vicinity of his head. Believe it or not, the punch — maybe the hardest I've ever unleashed in my convoluted life — landed right on the button, rocking Quarry's head back.

Staggered him.

His eyes opened wide.

Oh, gee-zus!

I moved in quickly, working the body, pummeling his ribs — bam, bam, bam, bam. Oh, yeah. I was putting the beatdown on him…except, the beating didn't faze him one bit. Despite my best efforts, he didn't go down. And my brain sent me a startling message:

Can ye light another candle for me, Mother? Methinks me gonna need it.

Have you ever been hit flush in the face with a two-by-four? Or have a grenade explode nearby, peppering your upper body? Or have a piano fall on you from four stories up? Did you ever wake up in a strange room and wonder what the hell you were doing there? Well, that was just round one, and now it was time for —

ROUND TWO

"Mind if I do some tricks?"

Oh, that jokester Quarry. I nodded, and he promptly wound his right arm in windmill fashion. My eyes hypnotically followed his right — and then he proceeded to casually slam three left jabs to my head.

Ah, the rest of the round is simply guesswork from here on out. I know I put the hurtin' on Quarry with four straight chins to his left, a cheekbone to his right, two bellies to his left, and a left eye to his right.

Never saw the punch which dropped me the first time. It exploded somewhere to the right of my temple. I remember trying to raise myself off the canvas and wondering how the hell I got there. I also remember my brain sending another message:

Mother? Mother? What's that you say, Mother? Don't get up? But I'm a Marine! We don't surrender. Hoooooo...rut-roh.

I struggled to my feet.

Ringside observers said the second devastating detonation came from a B-52 bomber. By this time, my arms felt like 50-pound weights were attached, legs nothing but rubber, no feeling whatsoever in my face.

A left hook separated my head from my body and sent me flying the second time. Bells went off and a door slammed in my face.

The Virgin Mary looked down upon me and shook her head in disgust.

I was on my hands and knees, searching for my head, when the referee stopped the fight.

As for my missing head? Still have the picture of Quarry cradling it in his gloved right hand.

He slowly raises me up, then clobbers me one last time for good measure.

THE END...ALMOST

Next thing I remember is regaining my senses in a car halfway to Cocoa. I was alive, but just barely. And there was Girard behind the wheel of my car. Laughing hysterically. He said something. Still couldn't hear for shit. This was gonna be one helluva long "What'd ya say?" trip home.

The dude's laughing again. Heard him loud and clear this time. "There I am, screamin' from our corner 'Stay down, you fool.' But no, why should you listen to me? Hell no, you've always got all the answers."

Try to focus my good eye. Try to comprehend what he's talking about.

More laughter from my manager. "Oh, my God, you're a sight for…" Girard can't finish.

"For wh-wh-wh-at?" I stammer.

"Sore eyes!" Girard's laughter is uncontrollable now.

I drain my beer. Open another. Put a flame to another cigarette.

"Anyway," Girard continues when he gets himself under control. "So down goes Smith! I'm screamin' from our corner for you to stay flat on your back. But no, you stumble to your feet as the ref's count reaches eight and — I kid you not, man — that's when Mike Quarry nails you with the flippin' kitchen sink."

My buddy Girard has a habit of speaking figuratively.

"Yessir, Champ," he said. "We did alright. We really showed them what stuff we're made of. We didn't run away from the big one. We did a real respectable job, that we did."

What's with this *we* stuff? So I asked him how *he* felt.

"Not bad at all. But when you were showering and Quarry's trainer was holding you steady so you wouldn't fall over and hurt yourself further, Quarry looked in and said someone your age shouldn't be in such bad shape."

He paused, taking a gulp of beer, then asked thoughtfully: "So, you gonna clean up your act and take better care of yourself, now?"

I nodded, fired up a cigarette, and reached for another beer.

KEEP YOUR ⬇⬇ UP
AND YOUR ⬆ OFF THE FLOOR

After the fight.
"I didn't really hit you that hard.
You need to get in better shape."

REDEMPTION

It was almost three months later when Mike Quarry once again climbed into the ring at the Orlando Sports Stadium. His opponent that Tuesday evening was Tony Santiago. Had talked about the bout over the weekend, letting June know that the newspaper wanted me to cover the fight. You know, duty calls, would be home late, yada, yada.

Life on the home front had rallied, somewhat. We were working out our difficulties — more to the point, working out her problems with my nightly misadventures, that is. But damned if she didn't surprise me, asking if she could accompany me to Orlando, having never witnessed a professional boxing match before. "Not to worry, hon," she said, the neighbors next door had already agreed to babysit our girls, Julie and Jill.

Ummm. Sure. Ya betcha.

No problem, dear.

The fight proved to be well worth the coverage; 10 rounds of solid, incessant brutality, my main man Mike Quarry winning on a split decision.

As I started to hustle off to Quarry's locker room in search of quotes for my story, June asked if she could meet Mike after he'd dressed and was ready to exit the arena.

Can do, dear. Quarry always liked to meet a lovely lady.

When he finally made it back to ringside, I made the introductions. Quarry politely stuck out his hand. Instead of accepting it, June reached out with both arms and hugged the bruised fighter, quickly planted a kiss on his cheek, and thanked Mike for beating the hell outta me.

For one of the few times in my life, I was speechless.

Still remember her parting words, which prompted Quarry into a fit of laughter. "Thank you, Mike," she said. "You'll never know just *how much* my husband deserved that beating. You are a godsend."

POSTSCRIPT

Turned out that the beating by Mike Quarry was worth it as I was cited for writing the best sports features of 1975 by the Florida Sports Writers Association, an honor I also won the previous year.

1975

All Things Evel

On my annual visit with my brother in Arizona. And not hiding from the life-threatening Covid-19 (yeah, I'm being sarcastic). I'm lounging on the patio. The coffee is Columbian and the book is *Evel*, yet another brilliant biography from Leigh Montville, former senior writer at *Sports Illustrated*.

In 1966, a young Montana cowboy made his first jump over rattlesnakes and tethered mountain lions on a Honda 250cc. After fits and starts, he barnstormed onto America's front pages on a Triumph Bonneville T120. Robert Craig Knievel would come to be known by thrill-seeking folks as Evel Knievel.

He captivated the nation and some parts of the world by roaring up and off and over long lines of cars and school buses and certain big ditches.

At first, folks are mildly amused by his antics. But then his notoriety soared out of sight amid a disastrous failure when he crashed trying to jump the fountains at Caesars Palace in Las Vegas. The 1967 New Year's Eve spectacle in Vegas was filmed by Linda Evans (yes, *that* Linda Evans). ABC's *Wide World of Sports* turned down live broadcast rights and ended up ruing that decision. They purchased the footage for a much higher fee and broadcasted nationwide.

Hey, if it bleeds it leads, right?

Watch the dramatic video of Knievel's spectacular slow-motion failure 53 years ago as he soars 140 feet, 11 inches — two inches short of what would have been his longest jump at that time — and crashes. These days you can YouTube it. Countless millions of viewers worldwide have — and cringed like all of us did back in the day. The dude was nuts and had a death wish. Indeed, he does.

Years afterward, when asked if he feared anything, Evel, a notorious woman-chaser, quipped: "Yes, VD."

You gotta love the dude's machismo.

He put on the showbiz with that slick white cape, aristocratic cane, white leathers studded with red-white-and-blue stars and bars, and nifty white boots. Add in his notorious Wild West upbringing, complete with petty theft and persistent run-ins with the local federales, heavy drinking, womanizing, motorcycle lunacy, and other missteps. Why, you'd think that with my drunken daredevil antics in the '60s and '70s Evel would've been one of my heroes. Things he did that should've appealed to me, interestingly, did not.

I thought it was every bit as absurd to parachute out of a perfectly good airplane as it was to steer a motorcycle at 90 miles per hour up a plywood ramp and go ass over teakettle above cars and buses or strapped to a rocket trying to fly over Idaho's Snake River Canyon like he did in September 1974.

So why am I telling you this? Did I ever tell you about the day I compared scars and broken bones with Evel Knievel? No? Well, let me do just that.

My job on that Florida Saturday afternoon in November 1975 was to coax some cool comments from His Evelness, then 37. "Something out of the ordinary" was how my boss put it. Which I figured would be easy enough because from all I'd come to know about the dude, everything Knievel said was out of the ordinary. My lead, which he called later to tell me was "kinda cool, in a humorous sorta way", read:

```
     Evel Knievel awoke
Saturday morning following
an all-night party at the
Stan Musial Hilton's
Upstairs Lounge, read the
obituary column in the St.
Petersburg Times and, not
seeing his name there, he
ate breakfast.
```

We met in the club's lobby. He limped toward me and I gulped coffee, blinking repeatedly trying to see through bloodshot eyes. Much to my surprise, he and I immediately bonded. Both of us were horribly hung over, which helped solidify the connection. Then we made way at the Belleair Biltmore Country Club to participate in the fifth annual U.S. Steel-American Cancer Society Celebrity Invitational golf tournament. The man loved golf.

"You play?" he asked.

I shrugged. Told him I'd never been bitten by the golf bug.

He nodded, then asked, "You ride?"

I smiled and said, "Hell on wheels. Had me a Honda 450, tricked out, high bars. Loved screamin' down that foot-wide asphalt extension on Illinois highways at 110 mph."

He nodded his approval, which prompted us hooking up later. But first he had to address his adoring fans, a more refined gathering than normal. No sleeveless denims, no bandannas or do-rags, no engineer boots among them. This group of well-wishers was adorned in high-quality golf apparel. Bankers, lawyers, a couple of mid-level local politicians, numerous refined ladies of various ages, and quite a few teenage hell-raisin' wannabes. At least a hundred crowded around the soiree's putting green.

All waiting to be entertained by the lead dog — he staking out his territory, laying down his own boundaries as only Evel Knievel always did.

"There isn't a man here I can't whip," he boasted, doing a quick scan of the crowd. "There isn't a man here I can't beat in arm wrestling. And see that Volkswagen? [Pointing to the Bug 200 feet away.] I can still jump my bike as far as that."

No challenges so far as the faithful nodded their agreement.

He smiled, knowing he had everyone in the palm of his hand. "Folks say I'm the white Muhammad Ali. Incidentally, a close friend of mine. But Ali's the black Evel Knievel," he said with a burst of laughter.

Enthralled by this reformed hubcap thief, self-professed bank robber, and bar fighter who softly waxed poetic with easygoing-yet-cocky rhetoric, you could almost hear the thoroughly captivated audience reverently stammer "Amen, brother. Amen" as they inched closer in hopes of getting an autograph.

But then some knucklehead reporter, with "Get him to say something out of the ordinary" echoing in his head, asked if His Evelness was bothered by accusations that he was nothing more than a con man, christened by his critics as "Ol' Broken Bones and Baloney".

The multitude murmured as if there was a disturbance in The Force, then lapsed into silence. Would there be violence? Would Knievel prove his fighting ability and take a swing at the idiot bleary-eyed reporter eagerly holding pen and notebook?

Nope.

Instead, Knievel kept his cool, quickly dampening the fiery sparks that momentarily danced in his eyes. He smiled and immediately declared: "I *am* the greatest con man alive. I want someone else to jump 14 buses and try to con their way through that."

His well-heeled followers broke out in laughter — The Force was restored! — and cheered him on.

"Yes, despite what some critics say, I can still put on a good show," said the man who did for motorcycles what the Surgeon General did for cigarettes. "But then again, I've been hurt so many damned times there comes a time when you've got to slow down. Truth is, I just don't want to be hurt anymore. I don't need it. I've paid the price for what I've accomplished. You can stare death in the face just so many times and get away with it."

He started to gracefully bow out of the conversation, but turned around and added, "You know, there comes a time when you can't beat that S.O.B. anymore. Death? He's a tough one."

Indeed. All total, 18 horrific crashes which, to no one's surprise, solidified his inclusion in *The Guinness Book of Records* with a stunning 433 bone fractures. And only God knows how many sutures and swatches of skin grafts. Fourteen times they cut him open. More than thirty-five screws and several plates held his bones together.

Somehow I thought it would be a good idea to tell Knievel that I damn well knew what crashes felt like. "Couple times on gravel," I said. "Shredded lots of skin on my left leg and cracked my left elbow. Still have no feeling in the kneecap. Got run off the road both times by an idiot driver."

He carefully studied the dead areas on my left cheek and exposed forearms, and asked, "How many times have you been forced to drop your bike? I mean, you've had no really *bad* crashes, though, right? Nothing like Caesars Palace or Tahoe Speedway?"

It was time to man-up. Knowing my two head-on auto accidents didn't count, I showed off the scars on my right forearm. "Got these crashing through the plate-glass window at a dance hall. I was the passenger on a buddy's bike; he couldn't stop in time on the ice and snow, and I went flying. Hurt like hell. Ended up getting arrested for trespassing; my buddy walked away scot-free."

That got a genuine smile because of his own brushes with The Man, but more to the point because both his forearms were a bizarre mix of skin grafts and surgical zippers.

"What about the nose? It's been busted more than once. You run into those high bars of yours?"

Now I felt like an idiot. "Boxing," I said. "Did a first-person story on what a professional fighter goes through in the ring. Climbed through the ropes to face light-heavyweight Mike Quarry, Jerry's little brother."

Knievel shook his head in disbelief. "You being just an amateur, right?"

"Yep, amateur all the way. Mike beat the hell outta me."

And so it went. Two knuckleheads comparing scars after dancing with the Devil. My five concussions surpassed his four, but his 35 broken bones dwarfed my 19. My five operations to repair leaps of uncommon sense are nothing compared to his.

I've fractured almost all of my ribs and right hip. But then, in our anatomical game of show and tell, he raised me three fractured pelvises, five fractured left femurs, three fractured lower vertebra...and a fractured skull.

At that point, I eyed my oft-broken knuckles and wrists (which amounted to a pair of deuces to his full house) and lifted my arms in surrender, damn well knowing when to fold 'em. Yet as I did so, grinned and uttered his most-oft-quoted machismo statement of all time: "Bones heal, pain is temporary, and chicks dig scars, right?"

He flashed that captivating smile, but then caught himself, as if having second thoughts. "You know, I *will* die someday," he said, offering his hand. "And when I do, I want to be known as a man whose word was as good as gold. Sure did appreciate your company."

POSTSCRIPT

Turns out His Evelness would have three more jumps left in him, the last on January 31, 1977, at Chicago's International Amphitheatre, jumping 90 feet over an open-top tank of water containing 13 sharks. Those Jaws musta rattled him a bit because he crashed, fracturing his collarbone and right arm, then retired to earn a couple of million dollars off the marketing of Evel Knievel dolls and other merchandise.

Battling diabetes and idiopathic pulmonary fibrosis, an incurable lung condition, the self-proclaimed "Last of the Gladiators" died on November 30, 2007. He was 69. Whisked away on a stretcher from his family home in Clearwater, Florida. Gasping for breath. Riding toward his final sunset. Dying as most of us had always imagined he would: in the back of an ambulance.

In Our Brother's Keeper, *I wrote about the death of my brother and how it affected our already screwed-up family. Since then I've been around the United States speaking freely and at length to groups of veterans and numerous other gatherings about that experience.*

Hard to believe, but there was a time when I never mentioned Jeff's death. Never even thought about it…or if I did, worked non-stop, racing the clock to outdistance the competition, hunting writing awards, begging for minuscule raises, loving my ever-growing family, and racing the demons to death as I buried memories in drunken blackouts and fistfights.

But healing always comes in stages. There must be that first cracking of the psyche which brings with it the awareness one needs to move forward in all areas of life. That first cracking took place for me while, of all things, covering Super Bowl X. But this story is not all about 30-year-old me. It's about a man I'd never met before but knew his story had to be told and then retold — a story for all generations.

1976

Rocky Bleier:
Purple Heart.
Bronze Star.
Pittsburgh Steeler.

"Welcome home, brother," I said, offering my right hand to 29-year-old Rocky Bleier.

The greeting was impulsive. And from Bleier's rather stunned expression, caught him off-guard. The ensuing silence left me momentarily tongue-tied. Recovered quickly, though, and said, "I was a Marine."

Grinned, then added, "Just wanted to thank you for being there" — *there* being the shitstorm that was Vietnam.

Bleier hesitated momentarily, released a soft sigh, then grabbed hold of my extended hand and shook it forcibly. Most of what followed seemed to transpire in a blur. His slight nod of gratitude. His motioning for me to take a seat at his table.

A rush of awkwardness, for I couldn't help but notice the quizzical look on his face — he probably wondering just where the hell the ensuing conversation was headed. Me equally as flummoxed and nervous. Guts twisted in knots, anxiety clawing at innards, and thoughts ricocheting off the darkest corners of my mind.

Jarred by remembrance of a brother lost forever...

Bleier's honed muscles in his neck and shoulders untightened. Then, after another momentary lapse of silence, his eyes cloudy now, he asked, "Nam?"

My response came in choppy starts and awkward stops. "We're a Marine Corps family. Dad fought at Tarawa, Guadalcanal, and Saipan in WWII. My younger brother, Joe, enlisted in 1969... I re-enlisted in '69 — same as Joe because..."

Felt like a dolt at that point. After all, this Pittsburgh running back was three days away from scampering onto the field, his AFC Champion Steelers facing the NFC Champion Dallas Cowboys in Super Bowl X.

And here I was dragging this Steeler down a dark and convoluted memory lane. That couldn't be good. Yet it seemed as if the entire Ft. Lauderdale banquet hall was suddenly blotted out. Everyone gone except for this solitary table jammed into the back corner of the massive interview room.

Couldn't help but question myself: *What the hell triggered my outburst?*

Bleier sat immobile.

Anxiety palpable, I looked deep into his eyes. What I saw was compassion. Pure and simple. So I stammered, "Yeah, both Joe and I wanted revenge, because our brother, Jeff…Foxtrot 2/4. I Corps. The DMZ. Killed. Ambush, you know, during '68 Tet."

Bleier took a deep breath, slowly released it, softening the moment. Bowed his head slightly, said he sympathized with our loss. "It's never easy…I know."

His smile much softer now, saying he'd like to know more about my brothers, our family, my health, how I came to be a sportswriter. "Don't worry," he said. "No hurry. I've been blessed. So…tell me."

Who was interviewing whom? There was an unexpected feeling of safety in Bleier's presence, so I shared a portion of our family grief. Fifteen or so minutes later I stopped talking. Decades later, I've come to view it as one of those preordained moments orchestrated by God. Necessary for me to begin looking for rainbows instead of peering over my shoulder at the nightmarish chaos of yesterday. Even though embarrassed by my torrent, oddly enough I felt as if a heavy load had been somewhat lifted.

Throughout it all, there had been no indication of disinterest or boredom on Rocky's part.

While an excess of 300 sportswriters and broadcasters crowded shoulder-to-shoulder around tables of the game's superstars — the noise level gradually ascending to that of a locomotive leaving the station — Bleier listened.

To me.

His eyes glistening.

Hands flat on the table.

Posture erect through most of the narration. Shoulders sagging during the tough spots, for he was quite familiar with such grief and sorrow. We were two strangers on a familiar journey through hell and damnation.

All of which gave me the courage to press on with the interview and have Bleier look back to yesteryear and share with our readers his astonishing journey to where he was today.

Sure, his teammates — most notably quarterback Terry Bradshaw, running back Franco Harris, and defensive stalwarts "Mean" Joe Greene and Jack Lambert — were exceedingly blessed with physical skills unsurpassed in this league of exceptional athletes. Yet none had overcome the nightmarish obstacles Bleier had.

After all, football is a mere game. But combat is a coin flip. Heads, you live. Tails, you're dead.

So, I gave him the opening he needed, saying: "Yeah, my brother Jeff was only nineteen. We lost him seventeen months before *you* got hit."

Can't begin to tell you how long the silence lasted. Certainly long enough to give y'all a short sampling of the man's background:

- 1968 Notre Dame graduate, a dependable yet anonymous running back with average speed and stature.
- Blue-collar roots, son of a father who owned and operated a tavern in a small, nondescript Wisconsin town.
- An overachiever, an NFL curiosity, which is why the Steelers didn't draft him until the next-to-last round in 1968 — the 417th selection, the 59th-best of 65 running backs selected that year.
- Somehow beating the odds by making the Steelers' 53-man roster, then appearing in the team's first 10 games, rushing for 107 yards.

But then Uncle Sam intervened in late November 1968. With four games still remaining in the Steelers' season, Bleier was inducted into the U.S. Army, endured boot camp and advanced infantry training, then ended up in Vietnam in May 1969. Just another anonymous Spec 4 humping a snub-nosed M79 grenade launcher through the boonies with Charlie Company, 4th Battalion, 31st Infantry Regiment.

Instead of running through opposing linemen, Bleier now was dodging AK-47 bullets and enemy mortar rounds from the North Vietnamese Army (NVA), near the southern end of I Corps, along a swath of hell that came to be known as Death Valley, east of Hiep Duc and thirty-five miles south of Danang.

Rocky's day of reckoning occurred on August 20, 1969, when he and twenty-four fellow grunts of Charlie Company, plus a command group of seven others, were ordered to retrieve the bodies of Bravo Company slain during an enemy ambush three days earlier. What they didn't know was a 130-man NVA force lay in wait for them. Bleier's unit was overrun, ambushed as it was slogging through a rice paddy.

"I remember trying to breech a load in my grenade launcher," says Bleier, "when I felt this dull thud in my left thigh; that was the first time I got hit. Blood gushed out of two holes, front and back."

A clean wound — ripping an inch-deep groove through flesh and muscle, miraculously avoiding bone.

Fellow soldiers not as lucky. Many killed, all others seriously wounded. One lay dead nearby, chest chewed up by machine-gun fire. So many swathed in crimson.

Screaming or silent. Forever silent. Panic, confusion, pandemonium, fear.

"About five hours later and still under attack, we hear a thud — a Chi-Com grenade" dropped in on Rocky and his hunkered-down mates. There is no escaping the panic. No running away to safety. The air above filled with enemy gunfire.

"So, I rolled to the right," Bleier says. "[The grenade] exploded in front of my right foot."

Knocked unconscious, both legs a confusion of blood, dirt, and sweat — his right foot twitching spasmodically — he is spared witnessing the ensuing carnage. A buddy is hit in the groin. Another's right lung is pierced. An NVA mortar round makes a direct hit on two other grunts. The radioman is shot through the throat. A crimson mist colored everything.

His voice now vague, haunted. "All I remember is laying there in water, gritting my teeth, ripping clumps of grass with my hands...and crying."

Nothing heroic about that, which is why Bleier prefers talking about his

NFL exploits, as innocuous as they might be.

But some memories never fade and psychological wounds never heal.

Eight hours later, a reinforced company fights its way through the NVA force, rescuing what is left of Charlie Company. Bleier is first carried out on a poncho by four soldiers. When it rips apart, he feels himself hoisted onto the back of another whose name he would never learn but who carries him the rest of the way to the 23rd Medical Company at LZ Baldy. Next stop, the 95th Evacuation Hospital at Danang, then later to Camp Oji Military Hospital in Tokyo.

"I was a cripple. No one spoke of me possibly playing football again," Bleier recalls. "Because everyone was worried about me even *walking* again."

But walk he did.

Though it took three painful years of recuperation. Numerous surgeries and plenty of prayers as he struggled to regain his footing. From crutches to cane. Baby steps at first. Then gradually learning how to run. His biggest fan, Steelers' owner Art Rooney Sr., refused to give up on Bleier, and assured Rocky that there would always be a place for him in the organization whenever he was able to return.

Most of all, Bleier never giving up on himself.

Miraculous, indeed. And now, in three days, Bleier would be playing a key role in his second Super Bowl. Not bad for a dude who could have just as easily bled to death in a rancid rice paddy in Southeast Asia.

Right, Rock?

Bleier flashes a tight smile. "It's an experience I'd like to forget," he says. "What I'm trying to do now is change the image. I don't want to be known as a Vietnam war hero. I'm now a football player. I'd like to blank Vietnam from my mind if I could."

That, of course, would be impossible because, fact is, he's got the scars to remind him: a four-inch puckered seam on his left thigh, and more than 100 shrapnel punctures running up and down his right leg. He'll also be the only player on the field Sunday wearing a 10-1/2 left shoe and a 10 right because that Chi-Com grenade blew one-half of a shoe size off his right foot.

Shortly before kickoff, Bleier would walk away from his teammates to find a secluded spot where he could privately thank a good friend for his assistance in the past, present, and future. What he said probably was something like this:

"Well, Lord, here we are again. Another Sunday with the breeze blowing, the flags flying, and all these people ready to enjoy themselves.

"Thanks for giving me another opportunity to be here...I'm not asking for us to win this game, or lose it...Help us to know our assignments, so we don't screw up...Let us have a good game, so I don't embarrass what I stand for — my religion, my school, my family, or myself...Thanks, Lord."

That said, Rocky Bleier — recipient of the Purple Heart and a Bronze Star with Combat V for heroism — felt a familiar chill run up and down his back, causing him to slowly raise his right hand and brush aside tears caused from the distinguishing strains of *The Star-Spangled Banner* being played before a packed house of more than 80,000 football fans. He then proceeded to run through the Dallas Cowboys en route to a 21-17 victory.

I'd like to believe that if y'all had listened to that game close enough, you might have heard a unified yet ghostly reverberation carried on a strong northeast wind caressing 58,318 headstones of our fellow American heroes whose starkly etched names would one day adorn the 140 black granite panels of the Vietnam Veterans Memorial in Washington, D.C., as the wind echoes:

"Welcome home, brother."

POSTSCRIPT

Since retiring from the Pittsburgh Steelers after the 1980 season, Bleier has toured the country as a motivational speaker, relating the hard lessons learned early in life that helped him overcome adversity.

He is also the author of *Fighting Back.* Robert Urich [*S.W.A.T.*; *Vega$*; *Spencer: For Hire*] portrayed him in *Fighting Back: The Rocky Bleier Story*, a 1980 made-for-television movie. Audiences have learned that ordinary people can, indeed, become extraordinary achievers. No one's ever gonna question his patriotism. But more important is this of which I am sure:

Rocky Bleier has no idea how much he helped me or has helped many others — and he'd probably be embarrassed to have it pointed out to him.

1976

The Ultimate American Hero

The voice on the other end of the line asked, "Mr. Smith?"

"Yes, sir," I hesitantly responded, expecting to be taken to task by yet another irate reader. But hey, we were selling papers, so I took the call.

"This is Jesse Owens. You were trying to reach me last week, I believe."

I was momentarily dumbfounded and immediately lost for words. My head was spinning ninety miles an hour.

Jesse Owens!

Finally caught my breath. "Ah, yes-yes-yessir. Sure do appreciate you returning my call, Mr. Owens."

A soft chuckle on the other end. "Jesse. Please, call me Jesse."

Back in the day, journalists were held captive by the telephone. Seemed like every time you stepped out of the office, that important call arrived. Which meant you dialed the number again, going through the same gate-keepers who once again promised that So-and-So would get back with you as soon as possible.

It was always a maddening game of telephone tag.

So, having placed a call to Owens' Arizona-based public relations firm (Jesse Owens, Inc.) in Phoenix days earlier, only to be told Jesse was out of the office on a speaking tour, I left my number with the receptionist who said she'd pass it on to her boss.

Bottom line: He was a very busy man. Constantly on the go. Promoting the upcoming Summer Olympics being held in Montreal, Quebec, Canada. He didn't know me from Adam; therefore, I seriously doubted he'd return my call. But when he did, he politely asked, "What can I help you with, Mr. Smith?"

I felt like standing and shouting to the newsroom that the greatest Olympic champion of all time — in my estimation, one of the greatest athletes on the face of the earth! — was on the phone with *me*.

Instead, I took a deep breath. "Want to let you know I sure do consider it an honor speaking with you again, sir."

He chuckled. "It's Jesse. I don't bite."

Here now, working on this book in 2020 and looking back on that call almost a half-century later, I'm left wondering at the noxious state of our country's race relations.

The term *racist* has been hijacked purely for political purposes, primarily being used to manipulate the weak-minded to kowtow to threats, and sow division, contempt, and unadulterated hatred between the races.

Being raised in a large Irish family of eight, where everyone worked together just to put food on the table, this old-timer finds it baffling. Then again, I've always been a simple dude. There was a time when we Irish were held in contempt. The same can be said for Italians, Jews, Mexicans, Chinese, Japanese, Vietnamese, blacks from wherever they come, and more.

Enduring stupidity along the way was a rite of passage. Only thing this country of ours ever guaranteed was the freedom to rise above our individual circumstances.

Which was to be…American.

Sadly enough, it seems as if certain segments of our society are only content when isolating groups into a skewed racial hierarchy which simply continues to nurture never-ending stigmas.

In my teens, had a black buddy named Roy O'Connor, a fellow high school athlete much more talented than the rest of us. I'd join him on weekends downtown and watch him pocket a lot of money shining shoes. Never saw him laugh so loud when I asked him how I could get a job like his, mesmerized as I was by how much coin he was making.

Once he stopped laughing, he said, "You just don't get it, do you, Smitty?"

Didn't then.

Don't now.

But now back to Jesse Owens.

Having twice shared conversations with Jesse on those long-ago days remains one of the greatest highlights of a career that necessitated nervously asking questions of individuals who had reached the stratosphere of sports stardom. Especially enjoyed it when their exploits collided with my passion for military history.

And Jesse Owens' feats certainly did just that.

It was Berlin in August.

The year, 1936.

The venue, the Olympics.

Hitler and his sycophants thought of that event as their personal showcase of Aryan racial supremacy. In his 1925 autobiographical manifesto *Mein Kampf*, Hitler dismissed blacks as a "primitive **semi-animal race** barely worth consideration". In Hitler's eyes, Owens was subhuman and "Americans should be ashamed of themselves, letting blacks win gold medals for them."

Oh, how the Nazis strutted and preened in the stands for all the world to see. One can imagine how Hitler and his inner circle snickered when a black man — worse, an American black man — came out to compete against Germany's top athletes. But their strutting, preening, and snickering soon turned to hisses of real hate when Owens won four gold medals.

But at 23, Jesse was the first American to figuratively kick Adolf Hitler in the ideological nuts by blitzing the Fuhrer's stomping grounds eight years before the Allied bombers finished the job by kicking his ass in World War II. How'd Jesse do it?

Jesse's record-shattering feats included a :10.3 100-meters, a 200-meters in :20.7, a long jump of 26 feet and 5 3/8-inches; and a :39.8 in the 400-meter relay with Ralph Metcalfe, Foy Draper, and Frank Wykoff.

Three years before Europe's darkest days would begin with Germany's 1939 invasion of Poland triggering World War II, in a stadium of 100,000, Hitler felt the race relations squeeze on his cojones as he desperately tried to ignore the four times Owens stood tallest on the podium, receiving the gold, and saluting his beloved Stars and Stripes while the U.S. National Anthem played loud and clear.

I'd first met Owens in 1975 when he spoke before a St. Petersburg, Florida, audience, a fundraiser on behalf of the U.S. Olympic Committee. It was an electrifying moment when the 61-year-old icon slowly rose to his feet and approached the microphone with a painful regimentation in his gait. The wrinkles, which ran a never-ending race across his face, glistened with sweat while the audience sat in awe, in silence, already mesmerized — no, hypnotized — by his presence.

Owens cleared his throat, broke into a tired, overworked smile, then slowly lifted his head and righted his fatigued body. And as his words flowed outward and through the hearts of those in attendance, it was difficult to stifle the chills racing throughout the body.

He spoke:

"The greatest moment came as we stood up there on that pedestal of victory for the long jump [on Aug. 4]."

He recounted his country's golden achievements. "And after we had knelt and received the wreath of victory from the German magnates, we stared toward the stands. And from a faraway distance we could hear the strains of *The Star-Spangled Banner*.

"And as the people in the stands stood, the Germans gave the Nazi salute. The Americans gave the American salute. And as we three [Luz Long, Germany, silver medal; Naoto

Tajima, Japan, bronze] on the pedestal turned our faces, I noticed the Stars and Stripes arising high and higher. And as our flag rose higher and higher, I realized my ambitions of eight years to become a member of Uncle Sam's Olympic team — to emerge a victor in the Olympic Games — had provided me with my greatest moment throughout my athletic career."

The audience, as countless thousands before them had done, then rose and cheered and shouted their appreciation. In unison clarifying the very essence of what makes ours the greatest country of all — One nation under God, indivisible, with liberty and justice to all.

I still get teary-eyed as Owens' voice resonates in my bank of memories.

Speaking with Owens a year later, I had been too awed by his Florida presentation to seek clarification of his opening remarks, highlighting his second gold medal instead of his first, an Olympic record :10.3 in the 100-meters the day before.

I also wanted to know more about his friendship with Luz Long, the archetypical blue-eyed, blond German runner-up in the long jump.

Highlighting the long jump presentation was what we'd today call a political no-brainer. After all, arguably the most famous of all '36 Olympic Games photos appearing on the front pages of U.S. newspapers and on highlight reels back in the day was that of an American saluting victoriously above Germany and Japan, with whom we were soon to be at war.

And because Owens was going from coast to coast raising funds for the U.S. Olympic Committee, he was intent to play the patriotic card, which always prompts the well-heeled to break the strong seals on their wallets.

"Funny now," Owens said in a hushed voice on the phone, toning down his nationalistic zeal a notch, pointing out how difficult it is "to make people understand that athletes have no prejudice or political beliefs. It's the skills which are important — not an individual's politics."

Proof of this, Owens said, was the fact that Luz Long became one of his best friends during and after the Berlin Games. Luz would join the German military as a sports instructor before being assigned to the Wehrmacht's 1st Parachute Division in defense of San Pietro Infine during the July 9, 1943, Allied invasion of Sicily. Grievously wounded on the second day of battle, Luz died three days later.

"My friend, Luz Long, was the first to congratulate me after I won the gold in the long jump," Owens said in a halting voice. "He held my arm aloft as the Germans screamed my name over and over. But people forget that scene... of my friend Luz."

Luz Long never allowed Hitler's vile racial sentiments to take root in his heart. The brotherhood fashioned amid Olympic competition endured. He and Owens continued to keep in touch in the years that followed, Luz writing his last letter in 1942, shortly after the U.S. declared war on Germany. What follows is a portion of that letter, provided by *HistoryNet.com*:

> I am here, Jesse, where it seems there is only the dry sand and the wet blood. I do not fear so much for myself, my friend Jesse, I fear

for my woman who is home, and my young son Karl [Kai], who has never really known his father. My heart tells me, if I be honest with you, that this is perhaps the last letter I shall ever write. If it is so, I ask you something. It is a something so very important to me. It is you go to Germany when this war done, someday find my Karl [Kai], and tell him about his father. Tell him, Jesse, what times were like when we not separated by war. I am saying — tell

```
him how things can be
between men on this
earth...
        Your brother, Luz.
```

"Now I see and write to his son often," Owens said in 1976. "Kai lives in Hamburg. He's 37 now — a chemical engineer."

Before I could further inquire about Luz's son, Owens changed directions, noting earlier I had called him a living legend, which he obviously enjoyed.

"Living legend — yes, that has a nice ring to it," he chuckled. "But there's a great deal of pressure which goes with it. You have to exceed to the wishes of all people; you give of your time and of all your energy. But I enjoy it."

Then an afterthought: "And it's a fact I've got more time than money."

Nothing startling about that. Upon his triumphant return home in 1936, he reminisced, "It became increasingly apparent that everyone was going to slap me on the back, want to shake my hand, or have me up to their suite. But no one was going to offer me a job."

So, in order to put food on the table for his wife, Ruth, and the first of their three daughters, Ohio State University's "Buckeye Bullet" grudgingly adjusted to his role as a curiosity by challenging small-time sprinters at local meets to races for cash, giving them a 10- to 20-yard head start before beating them with ease. He participated in stunt races against dogs, motorcycles, and even horses between doubleheaders of Negro League baseball games and toured with the famous Harlem Globetrotters.

It wasn't until the 1950s that financial prosperity finally smiled upon him, when he began giving inspirational speeches to Corporate America, and eventually on behalf of the U.S. Olympic Committee by personalizing the Olympic spirit.

"Hitler," Jesse Owens said. "People remember me as the man who put Hitler down. But I don't mind. You see, if they forget Hitler then they just might forget about me. And I'm just too damned old to be forgotten now."

I had one last question before he caught a plane to Detroit. The Fuhrer left the stadium after previously having shaken hands with two other gold medal winners. How'd he feel about Hitler declining to congratulate him?

There was a prolonged silence on the other end of the line. Exceedingly long, before Jesse Owens said, "I wasn't invited to shake hands with Hitler, but I wasn't invited to the White House to shake hands with [President Franklin Delano] Roosevelt, either."

With that, the legend abruptly yet politely broke off the conversation. "Gotta plane to catch," he said, once again leaving me at a loss for words, with lots of follow-up questions unasked.

POSTSCRIPT

Couldn't understand Jesse Owens being snubbed way back when. Still can't understand it today. Being snubbed by Roosevelt, the man holding the highest office of our country, was unconscionable.

I also find it deeply regrettable that I never had an opportunity to speak with Owens again. The son of a family of Oakville, Alabama, sharecroppers died at 66 on March 31, 1980, of lung cancer in Tucson, Arizona. He was a board member and former director of the Chicago Boys' Club, served as America's Ambassador of Sports for the

U.S. State Department, and as a U.S. Goodwill Ambassador.

In 1976, presidential recognition finally arrived with Gerald Ford awarding Owens the Presidential Medal of Freedom. In 1979 President Jimmy Carter bestowed the Olympic champion with the Living Legend Award. And in 1990 George H.W. Bush posthumously awarded him the Congressional Gold Medal.

As for the shrill race-baiters and duped haters in 2020, and the frightened sheep [Yeah, I'm talking about you, Justice Roberts] who fear offending the pretentious sensibilities of the morally misguided lest they pitch a fit — those standing idly by as ignorant anarchists march under the banner of social justice, rioting and burning cities in the most free nation in the history of mankind — I beg them to consider two things.

One: Before malcontents condemn others for their White Privilege, accusing them of being Nazi fascists, and before agitators accuse others of being Uncle Toms and traitors to their race, I first recommend they research history. Hitler, Stalin, Mao, Pol Pot, and a host of others of their genocidal ilk gained power through social terrorism by appropriating their country's educational system, eliminating dissent with censorship of the media and intimidation of free speech, inciting neighbor to spy upon neighbor, and pushing people to turn in relatives for not being politically correct, otherwise known as toeing the party line.

So, take a close look at them.

There they are.

Bitching and burning.

In reality, which side of history are these types of people on?

Two: I wish all to embrace these words of Jesse Owens:

"The only bond worth anything between human beings is their humanness....Find the good. It's all around you. Find it, showcase it, and you'll start believing in it."

God bless the United States of America.

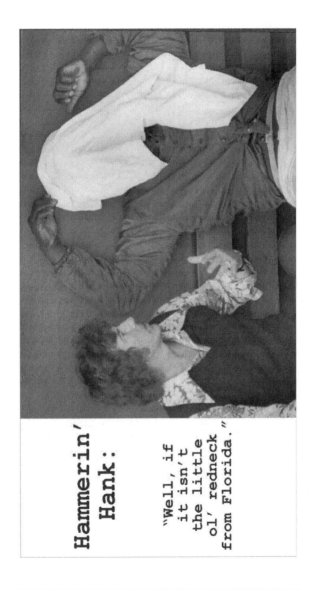

Hammerin' Hank:

"Well, if it isn't the little ol' redneck from Florida."

1976

"Say it ain't so, Hank."

It was a glorious day at the ol' ballyard. A homecoming of sorts, for I'd been on a four-year sabbatical from The Show, working in Florida — a state without a Major League franchise. That all changed with the move back north.

Which is how I came to be at Milwaukee's County Stadium on that Saturday afternoon, July 31, 1976.

Cleveland's sorrowful Indians were in town to play the home team, the woebegone Brewers, the least in the American League East. Mediocrity aside, it was a gorgeous day for baseball. Plenty of sunshine and temperature in the high seventies.

Yes, the stands were less than half full, attendance a dismal 18,175. Couldn't blame the fans for staying at home, though. That's what happens when your team has only won a meager 43 games while losing 54. More to the point, Wisconsin's rabid sports fans had already given up on their Brewers, shifting their focus to their NFL Green Bay Packers and the University of Wisconsin's football Badgers.

Didn't bother me none. Having just joined the staff of the *Racine Journal Times* as its sports editor/columnist, baseball was a breath of fresh air.

I was pumped.

"You gotta interview 'The Boomer'," quipped Paul Bodi, my right-hand man and moral compass, directing me toward Brewer first baseman George Scott. "He wears this cool necklace he says are the teeth from opposing teams' second basemen. He's quite the character, right up your alley."

Couldn't pass that up. And Boomer didn't disappoint, letting me know he wished he could return to Boston, the Red Sox having traded him to Milwaukee in 1971. Wishing aloud to play once again for a winning ballclub, he concluded our pregame conversation with "I'm sick of playing in Milwaukee."

He wasn't the only player who voiced those sentiments that day.

As I departed Scott's company and walked past the Brewers dugout, a familiar face noticed and snarled "Well, if it isn't the little ol' redneck from Florida," and quickly draped a towel over his head.

Ahhh, great to see you also, Hank.

Hank Aaron was still angry with me about a story I wrote twenty-eight months earlier in Florida at the Atlanta

Braves' spring training facility in West Palm Beach. On March 3, 1974, to be exact. Days of Lore, they were. When "Hammerin' Hank" was en route to breaking the immortal Babe Ruth's epic home run record of 714, which Aaron would eclipse a month later at Atlanta-Fulton County Stadium.

Granted, that 1974 interview Aaron had consented to was done with great reluctance. He was under extreme duress. Unbeknownst to most of my profession, Aaron was receiving anonymous hate mail and death threats from several terroristic lowlifes, news which the Braves organization hoped to keep from the public.

And Aaron blamed the media for fanning the flames of that antipathy.

Which is why, when I stumbled upon the story, Aaron downplayed the racist stupidity. Implying the hatred was generated by my profession's seemingly never-ending stories heralding his quest to shatter Ruth's record. Stories which somehow implied that poor ol' Babe's legacy was about to be disrespected by this black dude. Or words to that effect.

All of which prompted Aaron to say: "All you sportswriters can go to hell."

Which in turn raised more than a few eyebrows among my peers when it broke nationwide.

It's not like I was Woodward and Bernstein laying the groundwork for Tricky Dick's resignation. Hell, I was a blurry-eyed rookie sportswriter, reporting on a kids game played by adults. Aaron's job was to hit home runs. Mine was to fill in the gaps of his story between the time he arrived at the clubhouse until he departed for home.

Look, he was a national treasure, beloved by most from coast to coast. And the fact he was receiving random death threats and hate letters needed to be told — not hidden from view. Which is why Braves manager Eddie Mathews, who was deeply concerned for Aaron's welfare, talked him into sitting down with me for that first interview.

So, here we are twenty-eight months later in the heart of the Rust Belt. Aaron having signed a two-year contract with the Brewers after the Braves traded him to Milwaukee on November 2, 1974. But eroded by now was Aaron's capacity to generate massive fan interest producing fistfuls of dollars in stadium attendance. The only numbers that counted today were his age (42), last season's batting average (.233), and home run production (12).

In sarcastic columnist lingo, Hammerin' Hank had traded in his hammer for a putty knife. In journalistic jargon, he was "old news".

Besides, my only reasons for being at Milwaukee's County Stadium were to embrace my love for the game in general and to obtain column material from the Brewers' George Scott in particular. But when Hank threw that "little ol' redneck" barb at me, I wasn't pissed. I was embarrassed. So, I joined him in the dugout and started reminiscing about my passion for the game and my admiration of those I called "brothers" — him and Ernie Banks, Don Newcombe, and Roy Campanella. Only then did the tension between us diminish.

And what he would eventually share with me, what I assumed he had shared with numerous writers throughout this, his final curtain call, I also would assume to be old news.

Normally not a talkative individual, and certainly not one to ever pat himself on the back, I've always viewed Aaron as a quiet gentleman. So, once he'd patiently listened to my comments about "brothers" and how his old Milwaukee Braves had always broken my heart at Wrigley Field against my Chicago Cubs, Aaron pulled the towel off his head.

Which prompted me to inquire if he'd mind reflecting on his last five years in the Major Leagues. It was as if I'd poked him with a cattle prod. His eyes were riveted toward the infield. His elbows propped on his knees. With hands clasped, he said he wasn't in the mood for "needless pressuring". That caught me off-guard because I hadn't yet started pressuring him.

With eyes focused on a distant horizon I'd never be able to touch, he said, "I came here for only one reason and that was to play baseball. I signed a two-year contract and nothing else. The people here in Milwaukee will just have to realize that. What everyone doesn't realize is that my wife (Billye), my children, and all of my friends are in Atlanta."

There was a finality to that statement. Even more so, the next: "At the end of the season — well, that's it. I'm going back home. I'm going to Atlanta."

I remember thinking he'd surely said this numerous times to reporters during this dreadful season. So, I didn't miss a beat, asked him again if he'd mind reflecting on his last five years, three with the Braves and these last two with the Brewers.

"What are you getting at?" he said. His response had an obvious edge to it.

"Ah," I scrambled for a comeback. "I've seen how other of the game's greats, how they handled life as their skills slipped away. What I was wonderin' is —"

"I've been attacked by the experts of your profession," he fired back. "They've written it all about me — a lot of it bad, some of it good."

I tried another tack, asking what it was like viewing the final playing days of his old teammates Warren Spahn and Del Crandall, how they —

Again, he cut me off. "I never worried about what anyone else was doing. I was always too busy worrying about myself to care about them. I never gave them any thought."

What about some of the less-than-positive comments, the "bad press" he's received in quarters other than Milwaukee regarding his vanishing talents?

"Where did you see that?" he said bitterly, eyes flashing, and face drawn tight. When told in newspapers other than Midwest fan sheets, he stormed, "I don't pay any attention to that bull(bleep). I don't let those people bother me. All they write is bull(bleep) anyway. Nothing but (bleep). I have no reactions whatsoever to that (bleep)."

Ohh-kaaay! And as for the pressure of bowing out of the game with a loser?

"There's no pressure at all," was his curt response. "How much of a hassle do you think this is? It's just part of the job. No one can play under pressure and play as well as they can. Nothing bothers me. In fact, there's very few people who can say they've made as much money or had as much fun and enjoyed themselves as much as me. The pressure isn't there."

He smiled — for the very first time.

"I'm not as dumb as some would make me out to be," he said with a mischievous grin. "I'm not so dumb as to think I could have a good day every day. That's why I don't believe in playing under pressure. That's why I say most of those other writers are talking bull(bleep). Hell, they were talking the same bull(bleep) when I was averaging 44 homers a year. But they've had to learn a big lesson. You see, I'm a human being. They had to learn that."

Again, the smile and a short apology for exploding and going off on me like he had.

"I'm a 42-year-old human being," he said warmly. "If I was 25 years old and having the kind of season I had last year (batting .233 with only 12 homers) and this year (hitting .244 and only 10 home runs), why I'd go out and get a job doing what you guys do."

His laughter carried the length of the dugout. Again, the smile.

"All I can say at this time in my life is that what has happened to me is a result of God's given talent. Some of it I had to work on myself, but, still, I have no regrets."

Not even with me. We shook hands as I thanked him for allowing me the opportunity to do a little fence mending. And then I returned to nearby Racine to write the George Scott column.

Unbeknownst to me, everyone up here in this corner of the baseball world, foremost being then-Brewers president Bud Selig, took it for granted that Aaron would accept a front office position with the Brewers at season's end. Yes, there had been anonymous whispers that Hank was less than impressed with Milwaukee's ongoing ineptness, and its alleged unprofessionalism. Those grumblings, however, were simply viewed as meaningless rumor. Unverified, unconfirmed idle gossip, nothing more.

Truth be told, when I returned to the *Journal Times* sports department that Saturday afternoon, I started working on the George Scott column for Sunday morning's edition, transcribing the taped interview and checking my notes for accuracy.

Yep, totally unaware I was sitting on a blockbuster story.

I was typing the lead graph of the Scott column when Paul Bodi returned from County Stadium, saying he'd seen me in the dugout speaking with Aaron. And by the way, "What did the Hammer have to say?"

Once I told him Aaron more or less said "Happiness is Milwaukee in my rearview mirror", Bodi was incredulous. As I keyed my tape recorder to Aaron's epic revelations, staff photographer Bill Lizdas stopped by my desk and dropped off two pictures he'd taken earlier in the day — one of me sitting in the dugout beside Aaron, who had a towel draped over his head, the other showing us conversing amiably.

Never seen my consigliere run so fast in his life, hustling to editor Ted Findlay's office. Findlay, as hard-nosed and no-nonsense a mentor as either Bodi or I had ever had, at first was skeptical about the story until he had listened to the entire interview. In vintage *Washington Post* editor Ben Bradlee fashion, he grinned and exclaimed: "Run with it!"

It's not as if he said, "Beers are on me tonight, guys," but Paul and I both knew we'd be celebrating until the wee hours of the morning.

Yes, indeed, we'd done our job, and done it well. Teamwork, living up to our staff motto: Kicking ass and taking names!

And when the *Racine Journal Times* hit the front steps of our readers' homes the next morning, its front page was emblazoned with the screaming headline "Hank Aaron Says He's Leaving Milwaukee".

It was a stiff kick in the nuts to the Brewers' front office as well as its ever-faithful fan base.

In the blink of an eye, folks were ready to lynch the messenger.

As expected, the Brewers' hierarchy blew its cork, immediately scrambling to negate the story on Sunday. And who better to lead the charge than Hank Aaron, who told *Milwaukee Sentinel* writer Lou Chapman that I was "a (bleeping) liar. The only thing I said was I didn't know what I was going to do next year. That's all I said."

Wrong. And I had the taped conversation to prove it.

When approached by *The Associated Press'* Mike O'Brien, Aaron did not deny making the statements. Instead, he repeated almost word-for-word what I'd written. However, Aaron also said that statement shouldn't be interpreted to mean his plans definitely did not include the Brewers. In essence, covering his ass.

Not that it mattered. The story faded after a couple of days of Brewer non-denial denials. No thin skin on this reporter, so I hold no grudge against Aaron, one of the greatest baseball players I've ever seen. There was nothing majestic about his home runs. Instead of towering, high-arching moonshots dropping into the left-field bleachers or bullpens, what he launched over the course of 23 seasons were line drives, high-velocity rifle shots that ricocheted violently off whatever stood in their way. And before he was through, he would launch 755 of them.

My God, what an honor it was to both watch and sit down with him. To my lasting regret, I doubt the feeling was mutual.

POSTSCRIPT

Vindication of my story came two months later, on October 7, when Hank Aaron joined the Atlanta Braves' front office as Vice President and Director of Player Development, spending the next 13 years in that capacity before being named as the franchise's Senior Vice President in December 1989.

POST-POSTSCRIPT

They say it comes in threes, death.

- January 18, 2021: Don Sutton, L.A. Dodgers pitcher and Atlanta Braves announcer
- January 22, 2021: Henry Aaron, home run king
- January 23, 2021: Talk show host and pitchman, Larry King

Hank Aaron:
Dreamin' of
The Big ATL

1977

He Always
Had Our Back

This one's about Ted Findlay, my *capo di capi*, boss of bosses, the godfather of my journalism career — as I journey down Memory Lane to late January 1977.

It had been a rough month; January usually is. It begins with my birthday, another year older and deeper in debt. Then our wedding anniversary, complete with cute cards from friends and family that always begin the same way: "Can't believe June has stuck with you this long", this despite me treating my bride to an all-expense-paid trip to Southern California, celebrating our 10th anniversary.

Okay, okay — I was covering Super Bowl XI, Raiders versus the dog-meat Vikings in the Rose Bowl and thought June would enjoy the sunshine after suffering through a harsh Wisconsin winter. Which she did; thrilled to tears because she got to rub elbows with Frankie Avalon and Annette Funicello, Ricky and David Nelson, plus Andy Williams and Don Rickles.

She especially got a kick out of Rickles, who upon learning June was from the Midwest, said: "Here, let me make you feel at home — *mooooooo!*"

The Super Bowl gig was a gift from Ted Findlay, my boss and editor of the *Racine Journal Times*. Our relationship goes back to my first newspaper job in Belvidere, Illinois. Ted was the news editor at the nearby *Rockford Morning Star*. He was big-time, while I was the sports editor among a six-person news staff of the *Belvidere Daily Republican*. In hopes of making me a better reporter, I'd send clips to Ted every three weeks or so after he agreed to look over my work. He did a thorough job of this, using a red pen. I'd open the packet, only to believe he'd actually used the clips to wipe up blood from the floor of a nearby slaughterhouse.

Ted was like the Energizer Bunny; it was his recommendation that got me hired in July 1973 at Florida's *Cocoa TODAY*. He tried to hire me three years later in Racine, but I'd just accepted the job as the NFL Tampa Bay Buccaneers beat writer in St. Petersburg. He finally corralled me as the sports editor in Racine a year later. One of the perks of that job being the Super Bowl.

Ted's consigliere was Paul Bodi, my assistant sports editor, who in truth ran Racine's sports department. Hell, I had trouble managing myself, let alone a sports staff. So, between Findlay and Bodi, I became Hell on Wheels in Wisconsin's brisk clime — shaking things up in the surrounding area, mostly making a whole lotta folks uncomfortable, if not downright angry, something I seem to be very good at.

My 366-day joyride through America's Dairyland began my first week on the job in August 1976, visiting County Stadium and reuniting with Henry Aaron, then took on a terrorist bent in late November when I compiled a futuristic feature geared to the movie *Two Minute Warning* that was being shown at a local theater.

Seemed like a good idea at the time — how easy it would be for an assassin to slip undetected into Chicago's Soldier

Field, carrying with him a briefcase in which is a disassembled high-powered rifle. Following the movie's storyline, the game is deadlocked 10-10 in the fourth quarter, and the hated Green Bay Packers are threatening to score, having moved down the field on the strength of running back Eric Torkelson to the Bears' 34-yard-line.

As the clock ticks down to 0:53, the assassin quickly assembles his weapon, and takes aim.

To give our readers a visual picture of what is about to transpire, Bodi has graphically laid a gunsight's bull's-eye over a huge, three-column file photo of Torkelson fumbling the ball. Bodi's graphic bull's-eye is a beauty to behold — it being dead-center in the 6 of Torkelson's number 26 that adorns his jersey. Swear to God, it appears as if Torkelson's been shot.

Whoa, the story and accompanying graphic cause a firestorm throughout the region. Lessons learned: Don't kick the hornets' nest that is the Packer faithful. Ditto the Vikings' faithful, regardless how pathetic they would play 40-some-odd days later in SB XI.

With all those embers still glowing, the teachers union in Racine County threatened to strike a mere 10 days after the Vikings flushed themselves down the toilet.

My job was that of a first responder, providing commentary — what some might label as my "twisted opinion" of the local landscape. I was Sean Hannity before he landed at Fox News. And almost as controversial. But no matter how much anger was directed at the *Journal Times*, Findlay and Bodi were always guarding my flanks. Granted, it's not like I had free rein, and there were times when Findlay would ask,

"What was your second option?" Bodi would sometimes cringe and say, "You gotta be kidding me, right?"

But for the most part, they covered my back, allowing me to roam the twisted, dark corridors of my journalistic hero, Hunter S. Thompson.

So, where is this diatribe headed? To a watering hole, of course.

Regarding the teachers strike, I wrote a scathing column condemning the teachers, who I lambasted for holding the county's students hostage — blackmailing the school board, holding education over the heads of the brass like a big sword.

Of note, I had skin in this game of balls and a strike. Two daughters, the oldest in third grade, the youngest in first — both products of Florida's lackadaisical educational system. Both had difficulty reading and writing. Thus, Racine's teachers had pinched a nerve. My response was to tear the union a new one. You'd have sworn I'd just unleashed Hell itself.

All of which found Findlay (the first time he'd ever joined us at a bar), Bodi (always my drinking sidekick), Dick Pufall (our massively built college writer, easily the biggest of our motley crew), and me at a local tavern one afternoon, merrily imbibing numerous pitchers of Milwaukee's finest, basking in the glow of victory. Minding our own business. Bothering no one.

Aaaahhhh…no one 'cept the three big-bodied local high school football coaches bellied up at the bar. They glared at us, sucked down more bottles of beer, then glared at us some more.

Finally, one of them said, "I know you. Yer da guy from da paper. Wrote that crap about us going on strike."

Please note that for your benefit I've cleaned up his comment quite a bit.

Nonetheless, the challenge had been issued, the gauntlet thrown down. I eyed the three dudes, knowing if I were to respond, I would end up getting my ass kicked. And because my boss and his right-hand man were with me...well, that adage about "discretion being the better part of valor" crept into my mind. So, I just flashed the three meatheads a sarcastic smile and let the moment pass.

All would have ended well had not one of the thugs then pointed a meaty finger at me and growled, "You're the asshole who put that bull's-eye on Torkelson."

Which prompted me to step into the aisle and respond, "Yeah, and I'll put a friggin' bull's-eye on you if you don't back off."

My, my...I'd just written another check with my mouth that my ass couldn't possibly cash. But then I saw the three dudes hesitate. Had little ol' me called their bluff? That's when I noticed their collective eyes darting to my left and right, where Batman and Robin stood at the ready, defiantly guarding my flanks.

Paul Bodi — fists clenched, wondering what the hell he had just stepped into, but cowboying up, nonetheless. Always walking point on patrol, his head on a swivel.

And Ted Findlay — following suit, all 120 pounds of him; the Don Knotts of the newspaper industry, a banty rooster's banty rooster. Say whatever you will about his diminutive size, the man had cojones, which is why I still consider him the boss of all bosses.

Bottom line: It's easy to go to war with cornerstones like that at your side.

POSTSCRIPT

Those three thuggish coaches exited the bar grumbling, eyes aglow, but greatly subdued as if they'd just seen the ghosts of Christmas past. Paul Bodi grew accustomed to my penchant for walking barefoot along life's razor's edge, hiring me 12 years later as his sports columnist at the *Gwinnett Daily News*. And there will be more of that later, too.

As for Ted Findlay? He, too, would continue to ascend journalism's corporate ladder, eventually landing in Kansas City to run Universal Press Syndicate, and convincing me to leave the *Chicago Tribune* in 1980 to become the *Kansas City Times* sports editor.

Forever the mentor of vast wisdom and profound grace, Ted never ever went drinking with any of us again.

1977

Give 'Em Hell, Al!

Never gave much thought to college basketball. Had covered plenty of games earlier in my career but could never quite wrap my head around it. Forget the team concept — it was one shooting star and four stiffs. Considered covering the sport a half notch or so above synchronized swimming.

Granted, basketball was a bit more engaging than water sports. Eight lean, towering dudes jump high into the air after two smaller guys take turns dribbling up and down the court before passing the ball. Back in the day there was no 30-second shot clock, so if you were watching a Dean Smith-coached North Carolina team run its four-corners offense (yawn), you had plenty of time to visit the restroom and wash your hands at your leisure, then mosey over to the concession stand and stand in a long line for a hot dog and Coke — and you'd still miss absolutely nothing.

Fans in Chapel Hill sure did love it, but I'd rather watch an engaging chess match. Now, that's drama.

But until I'd landed in Racine, Wisconsin, every college hoops coach I'd run across had the personality of a life insurance salesmen: *Why yes, Mr. Smith, I know you're only thirty-one, but the Grim Reaper eagerly awaits you, so show love for your wife and kiddies. Sign here. Now, don't you feel better? I'm sure your wife does.*

But that opinion got a shake-up the moment I first met Marquette

University's Al McGuire. He stunned
the college basketball world midway
through the 1976-77 season when he
announced his retiring at season's end.

Indeed, the game had gradually
taken its toll on the brash, gifted lad
from the Bronx. From high school
stardom at St. John's Prep, to four years
of accolades at St. John's University,
then four more years grinding it out on
the professional circuit with the NBA's
New York Knicks. He turned to
coaching in 1957 and worked his magic
at Belmont Abbey in North Carolina
before taking the helm at Milwaukee's
Marquette in 1964.

"That's a lot of socks and jocks," he
joked. But it was now time to step aside.

Rick Majerus was an assistant coach
and close confidant under McGuire
during Marquette's epic 1976-77 NCAA
title run. He later coached University of
Utah to the 1998 NCAA finals, losing to

Kentucky. He told ESPN in 2001, "In the end, coaching got to [McGuire]. He told me he didn't like going to practice anymore. He said he's getting older and the kids are staying the same age…"

Those of us who followed Marquette during its journey to the '77 Final Four would have had a good laugh had Majerus shared that with us at the time because we damn well believed Al McGuire had never truly grown up.

To hear Al speak, you'd swear he was still that cocksure young ruffian from the Bronx.

At least, that's how he struck me on our first meeting. Confident to the point of being almost cavalier, a word that would've made him cringe. He was one hundred percent city backstreet wrapped in a slick black suit. To be sure, here was a coach who wouldn't put me to sleep when he spoke. Half raucous, half riotous. He changed my perspective about the game. Actually, he spoiled me. Had never met anyone else who could command my attention full time until years later meeting Jim Valvano.

But then Jimmy V died too soon, cancer taking him in April 1993, again leaving me with a ho-hum void that was hard to fill.

I first met McGuire in late December 1976, at the urging of Paul Bodi, my assistant sports editor at the *Racine Journal Times*. Paul spent most of his time running the department and keeping me between the white lines.

He barked.

I jumped.

But when he said there was a helluva story awaiting me up the road in Milwaukee on West Wisconsin Avenue, I smelled a rat.

And that would be? says I.

Marquette basketball says he.

Ah, geez, sure would like to accommodate you, boss, but I'm getting a lobotomy this afternoon says me.

Ol' Mr. Bodi wasn't buying it. Said he'd already set up the interview; McGuire would be waiting in the gym for me at two o'clock. Sharp. Said I'd better not keep the Big Man waiting.

So I made the drive, Bodi's words still ringing in my ears: McGuire's unlike any coach you've ever met.

He's a man after your own heart. I mean, he's more entertainer than coach, yet is still better skilled at molding a team to his style of play than 99 percent of the rest of the coaches in the country.

You're gonna love the guy.

He's a street dude.

He's a winner.

Made the drive to Milwaukee, pulled onto 16th Street, parked, and made way down the steps inside the university's U.S. Navy ROTC building. Walked into the old gymnasium to be greeted by this curly-haired, 48-year-old Irish-Catholic with a Three-Card Monte smile.

Briefly checked out his bio; his winning percentage was staggering. In the previous twelve seasons with the Warriors, McGuire's won-lost record was a phenomenal 270-73. Marquette was a perennial power, the greatness of which is only measured when a team is selected to appear in the season-ending 32-team NCAA Tournament, or March Madness as it has come to be called.

To say McGuire-coached Marquette teams measured up to those elite standards is an understatement. His Warriors were presently on a 10-year postseason-tournament roll — National Invitation Tournament runner-up, losing the title to Southern Illinois in 1966-67; making it to the NCAA Mideast regionals the next two years; NIT champions in 1969-70, beating St. John's,

65-53; again making the NCAA Mideast regionals the next three years; getting beat by North Carolina State, 76-64, in the NCAA championship game in 1973-74; then again making it to the NCAA Mideast regionals the past two seasons.

Damn, I was in the presence of greatness. Instantly took a liking to the gent; was engulfed by his charisma. Had trouble at first figuring out what he was talking about. He had his own lexicon, that's for sure.

Upon complimenting McGuire on his success, his response was baffling. "Seashells and balloons," he quipped, his accent clearly honed on the mean streets of New York City.

Seashells and balloons? In McGuire-speak that was victory and happiness.

Over the next three months of reporting on the team, I was introduced to other McGuire-isms. A couple of my favorites: a Dunkirk was an extremely poor performance; memos and pipes were university administrators and professors; and congratulate the temporary meant live for the moment.

What I knew without fail from the moment I met him was that all I had to do was hit the red button on the tape recorder, ask a simple question, and I was off to the races — hell, the stories seemed to write themselves.

In return, in March 1977, he took his ever-faithful Marquette fans on the ride of a lifetime to what McGuire called "The Big Dance": the NCAA Final Four held in Atlanta at The Omni. As the proverbial fly on the wall, I witnessed the Warriors' stunning championship victory over North Carolina.

Once the fans ceased celebrating, I watched a lone silhouette making his way toward the departure gate at Atlanta-Hartsfield Airport to await a flight back to Milwaukee.

It was Al McGuire. The man I'd come to love and admire.

Oh, what a fitting departure it was — what every great actor/entertainer wishes for, bowing one last time before gracefully exiting in Oscar-worthy fashion, basking in the glow, love, and applause of an SRO audience.

It played out in this fashion...

March 26, NCAA SemiFinals; Marquette vs. North Carolina-Charlotte

I've got the best seat in the house. Mid-court, press row, last seat on the left, right beside the Marquette bench. Eyes darting between McGuire and courtside comings and goings. Every moment recorded mentally, to be replayed over and over, ever thankful for the memories.

Marquette starts off strong, killing University of North Carolina-Charlotte (UNCC), holding a 23-9 lead with less than seven minutes left in the first half. Under ordinary circumstances, McGuire would say the opposition was a *cupcake* (easy opponent). Ah, not so quick, Coach. UNCC has this *aircraft carrier* (big center) dude named Cedrick "Cornbread" Maxwell, who's a shot-blocking, clutch-scoring demon, and closes his team's deficit to 25-22 at the half. Yikes…

Gotta pause here, filling you in on what kind of team — with the emphasis on *team* — McGuire has brought to this Final Four tourney being held in Atlanta, a city Sherman once torched.

The other three survivors from the original 32-team, single-elimination field have arrived here on the strength of individual stars.

Studs that will later have NBA teams drooling to acquire them.

University of North Carolina-Charlotte's 49ers have Cornbread Maxwell and Lew Massey.

North Carolina's Tar Heels have first-team All-American Phil Ford, Mike O'Koren, and Walter Davis.

University of Nevada-Las Vegas' Runnin' Rebels have Reggie Theus and Eddie Owens.

But the Marquette Warriors? Compared to the other teams, this is a squad best known for its anonymity — a band of playground hooligans and part-inner-city "got no idea where my next meal is coming from" street urchins. No individual star. Hell, even McGuire has difficulty attaching correct names to the right faces. There's —

Bo Ellis: Six-foot-nine senior forward from Chicago's south side. "Gangs, drugs, killing — the streets,"

Ellis would tell me during that initial trip to Marquette four months earlier. "When the shooting was going on, I was across the street (72nd Street) playing ball in Hamilton Park. It was the usual growing up; an all-black neighborhood, an all-black (Chicago Parker) high school, and all my friends were black. That's been the biggest change for me here. I got to meet a lot of different people, new friends."

Butch Lee: Six-foot-one junior guard from the heart of New York's 153rd Street Harlem ghetto. "When I recruited Butch, I took an FBI man along with me for the ride," McGuire says, enjoying the moment. "See, I usually took $150 when I was traveling. It's the kind of neighborhood that before I got out of the car, I took $125 out of my wallet and put it in my sock. See, normally, if a guy's gonna mug you, he only wants enough for a hit. And I believed $25 was the going rate for a hit at that time."

Bernard Toone: Six-foot-nine sophomore forward from Yonkers, New York. His claim to fame happened during halftime of the Warriors' first-round Midwest Regional game against Cincinnati. After twice bitching and moaning to McGuire that he hadn't gotten enough playing time, Toone would end up getting punched by McGuire, then wrestled to the floor in the team's locker room.

Always the dictator, the absolute King of his Hoops Kingdom, McGuire had no time for petty debates. There was no room on his team for selfish individualism.

So, down goes Toone, which sent a message to the rest of his players: Get your asses in gear and play ball, my kind of ball. The six-foot-two McGuire would later joke, "The other team is in their locker room talking strategy and X's and O's, and we're having a rumble." McGuire would later credit the Toone confrontation for helping his team on this title run. They've been kickin' ass ever since.

Jim Boylan: Six-foot-two junior point guard from Jersey City, New Jersey. He liked to reminisce about his playground pickup games in a decaying neighborhood that led to wild afternoons sucking down beer at a bar called DJ's.

Jerome Whitehead: Six-foot-ten junior center from Waukegan, Illinois. In McGuire terminology, Whitehead was "a cloud piercer". That ability to soar high in the air would be the deciding factor in events to come.

McGuire's other pieces of the puzzle: Bill Neary, Craig Butrym, Gary Rosenberger, Jim Dudley, and Robert Byrd; what the coach referred to as his "scrambled eggs" — those he kept shifting in and out to disrupt the opposition to change the rhythm of the game. Every player, a role to play. Such is McGuire's concept of perfection…

And now we return to the UNCC semifinal. As McGuire later told me, UNCC closing the gap "is what saved us. They (the 49ers) started to go uptown, and we were fudging. When the Queen Mary is going to be turned, one little bump starts it. You gotta flow inside a game — I don't want to conduct a clinic — you gotta flow."

Translation: You're pissin' the game away, guys. Time to tighten up. Man-up. Kick some ass. You own this street, so start actin' like it, damn it!

Problem was, Marquette didn't start flowing until the game's final 10 minutes. And most of it, unexpectedly, came from Jerome Whitehead, who almost single-handedly kept the Warriors alive by scoring 10 of his team's final 15 points.

But with the clock ticking down, it looked as if the 49ers were headed to Monday night's championship game, taking a 47-44 lead with 1:41 remaining as UNCC's Melvin Watkins makes both free throws after being fouled.

That's when McGuire jumped to his feet, made a sharp right-hand turn toward press row and unleashed a violent dropkick — missing the intended target, the wooden bleacher-seat support directly in front of me, instead nailing the metal post supporting the press table.

I can still hear his agonized scream. Still can see him shaking his head as he says, "Aw shit, there goes my (bleepin') golf game." And then he calmly limped back to his seat. It was one of those Kodak moments forever engraved on my mind because what both of us missed was Butch Lee nailing a 22-foot jumper from atop the circle to cut UNCC's lead to 47-46 with less than a minute left.

Seconds dwindling away.

Butch Lee hits another jumper; Marquette retakes the lead, up by one.

Gary Rosenberger gets fouled driving to the basket, misses the first.

UNCC calls timeout!

All eyes are on McGuire as his players huddle around him. He's slapping Rosenberger on the arm. *McGuire's finally gone nuts!*

Rosenberger makes the second free throw. Marquette now up by two with 0:13 left on the clock!

UNCC's Cornbread Maxwell drives the middle. Makes an unbelievable, off-balance shot to knot the game 49-49.

Three seconds left to play!

Marquette has one desperation chance to put the game away — a full-court, high-arching, inbounds pass from Butch Lee toward the Warriors' basket.

Ball sails toward Bo Ellis and UNCC's Maxwell.

Their bodies arch high into the air at the foul line.

Two seconds!

Ball glances off Ellis' fingers —

Through Maxwell's outstretched hands —

To Jerome Whitehead!

Maxwell turns and confronts Whitehead.

Whitehead goes for the dunk.

Maxwell gets a hand on the ball!

It ricochets against the backboard!

Against the rim!

Then drops through the net a fraction of a nanosecond before time expires.

Marquette wins, 51-49!

The noise in the arena is deafening. Chaos follows. McGuire runs onto the court only to be embraced by Butch Lee as Whitehead appears stunned.

Whitehead would later say, "When I made the shot, I hear the buzzer and then look at the clock. But the clock still shows the score 49-49."

Wait — did Whitehead's shot count?

The refs huddle with the official timekeeper, Larry Carter, seeking clarification that Whitehead's shot had, indeed, beaten the buzzer. Referee Paul Gaven asks Carter where the ball was when the buzzer sounded. "In the basket," Carter replies. Gaven repeats the question, and again Carter says, "In the basket!"

McGuire turns to the crowd, smiling magnanimously, his arms lifted high, confirming Marquette's victory!

In the media crush following the dramatic finish, McGuire explained what was happening with the slapping of Rosenberger. "Everyone thought I was going into my crazy act. Lee (Rose, UNCC coach) called time to ice Rosey. I just wanted to loosen him up."

As for Jerome Whitehead's last-second heroics, McGuire tries his damnedest to burnish his team concept, passing out kudos right and left. But he knows there's no avoiding the obvious. "And this young man on my left is…" and he suddenly can't put a name to a face, and stares blankly at the hero of the moment.

Whitehead then makes another game-saving assist. "Jerome Whitehead, coach. I'm Jerome Whitehead."

McGuire quickly recovers his wits, commending his star center, who on this night had doubled his scoring average with a game-high 21 points. "Jerome finally got his day in the sun. Yes, he finally had his day."

And just like that, Marquette would face Dean Smith's North Carolina Tar Heels on Monday night.

March 28, NCAA Final: Marquette vs. North Carolina

Admittedly, until this night arrived, there had only been two refrains that brought tears to my eyes: *The Marine Corps Hymn* and *The Star-Spangled Banner*. But shortly before the opening jump ball, the Marquette band started a bass-drum thumping, brass-horn blaring, Warriors-fan rhapsody that gave me the goosebumps and sniffles.

So, Monday came.

The final game of the tournament and his team is in it.

"Give 'em hell, Al," the crowd roared in synch with the band and screamed over and over and over, each chant more thunderous than the previous, until Al McGuire, always the entertainer, finally pulls back the curtain and strides onto the biggest college basketball stage of all. Mere seconds before the game — his final game — gets underway.

And, by God, he was going to milk the moment for all it was worth. After all, as he so often had said, "I don't really know what it's like not to be a celebrity. I like to have smoke rings blown at me."

In the same breath, having suffered alongside his teams coming up short in eight previous trips to the NCAA Tournament, he admitted, "I've always been the bridesmaid. More like a lunch pail, tin-hat type of person. I never thought I'd really win. But I'm a positive thinker, so I always thought I'd come in second."

But there would be no second-place finish on this night. The Warriors were as magical as was the moment. McGuire's throng of streetwise survivors could do no wrong. Even when Dean Smith's Tar Heels took a 45-43 second-half lead with 13:48 remaining and then went into their vaunted four-corners offense, Marquette took away the backdoor play with a sagging defense.

The four-corners proved to be the Tar Heels' undoing, for they would only score four more points in the next twelve minutes.

As McGuire would say, "In order to kill the animal, you have to cut off his head." The animal in this instance was Tar Heels All-American Phil Ford. Marquette's Butch Lee would harry Ford all night and hold him to a mere six points.

All of which, in McGuire terminology, led to the "carnival gates being closed". And with the scoreboard showing the Warriors leading 67-59, the game's final five seconds ticked off. The last jig of the Big Dance was finally his.

No more bridesmaid.

No more enduring that which he dreaded most — being an also-ran, an afterthought.

In his own words, "Being a professional loser."

As those final seconds ticked away, Al McGuire covered his face with his hands and cried. Those of us who cheered for him, now cried with him.

And Now, the Rest of the Story…

Heading home, I was sitting on a bench in the far corner of the outbound passenger terminal at Atlanta-Hartsfield Airport. Overnight gym bag at my feet contained five of the airport's last beers, courtesy of Chuck Baumgardner — a drinking man's dream of a bartender.

"Never seen anything like this," he'd told me earlier, as the clock swung past midnight, Tuesday morning. "I usually close this place down at 11 o'clock. But for winners, I make exceptions. You people must be from Milwaukee, 'cause you've drunk up the airport."

So there I sat, with the sixth of the last beers in hand, figuring Al McGuire would be making his way toward the Milwaukee flight terminal anytime now. Figured he'd be in dire need of a beer — and would know where to find one.

Didn't have to wait long. Saw his silhouette easing down the walkway. He spotted me holding aloft a cold one. Obviously drained of further emotion, he gave a slight smile and took a seat. Again, one of those Kodak moments forever engrained. Small talk between beers. Street language, some of it guttural, most of it stuff ordinary folks wouldn't or couldn't understand. Mouthfuls of McGuire-isms.

"Winning is only important in surgery and war.

"I'm the boss. The players know it. There's give and take, but in the end, I'm a dictator.

"Colorful? It would be hard to be this way if I was a loser."

Again, referencing the roughhousing he'd given Bernard Toone sixteen days earlier in the opening round of the Midwest Regional against Cincinnati.

Sure, yeah, of course. But I couldn't recall the last time a dictator had peacefully abdicated his throne. Also knew there be no more *white knucklers* or *sand fights* (close games) of his to report on. Couldn't help feeling sad about that, how folks no longer could look forward to being entertained by McGuire's courtside antics. Figured he would gravitate to the world of broadcasting, but didn't raise the subject. Didn't think this was the time or place. To borrow one of his McGuire-isms, thought this was the perfect time to *go barefoot in the wet grass* — enjoy the moment.

Nonetheless, thought the game would never be the same, not without him leaping from the bench, turning to the crowd, and placing his fingers to his forehead in bafflement by a referee's errant call. Or dropping to his knees, begging a referee, "Take my car! My home! Take my wife! But don't steal the game from me."

Was wrong, of course. Had no way of knowing that within a year McGuire would sign the big contract with NBC and join the incomparable duo of Billy Packer and Dick Enberg on national college basketball broadcasts. As former Marquette assistant Rick Majerus told ESPN in 2001, broadcasting brought a nice dimension to McGuire's life, giving the entire country a taste of his wit and wisdom — not just a handful of sportswriters in select gymnasiums.

"Al spoke to the common guy. He didn't complicate the game," said Majerus. "He and Billy Packer usually took polarized positions and Dick Enberg was the master referee during their days at NBC."

For the moment, a thoroughly exhausted McGuire shifted his weight on a cold Atlanta-airport bench along an almost vacant walkway, awaiting what he thought would be the last of 20 arduous yet successful years of red-eye flights. He closed his eyes and popped the top of another beer. He sighed, then absently repeated what he'd said so many times in the past:

"You know, it's a simple game. Most of the time it's like kindergarten. When you have the ball, you're king. But when I have it, I am king. And when you dribble, you are king. But when you stop, I am king."

I'm drinkin' and thinkin', "Damn, I love this guy. He speaks with exclamation points."

McGuire slowly twists his head, working out the kinks, the tightness, the intense pressure from what seems like a lifetime of coaching. He smiles and says, "You know, what I said after the game is still here, right now. I'm thinking of all the locker rooms, the dirty jocks, my pals, and things a New York street fighter knows when growing up. It doesn't seem real."

He pauses, searching to pull out one final and fitting McGuire-ism. Seems almost Biblical: "My day is over."

We shake hands, he slowly rises, and starts to walk away to grab that red-eye flight back home. I say, "Seashells and balloons, right, coach?"

He looks over his shoulder, once again flashing that Three-card Monte smile, nodding in agreement. Yeah, seashells and balloons!

That was the last time I was in the company of Al McGuire. I enjoyed his stories and he enjoyed mine. We were two ships passing in the night. He, the most quotable coach I'd ever run across, moving on up to the NBC broadcasting arena; me, going in search of other storied coaches, athletes, and eventually real warriors and battlefields that struck my fancy.

On January 26, 2001, a dismal Friday morning, Al McGuire died at 72, in Brookfield, Wisconsin. When he retired from television broadcasting the previous March, he said he had a form of anemia, declining to give more details because "Everybody will cry".

Which is exactly what I did when I heard the news.

1983

Prelude to a Life Worth Living

After almost three months at Brawner's Psychiatric/Addiction Recovery Center in northwest Atlanta, my life underwent a needfully uncompromising transformation in late February 1983 and for the first time since 1968, I was dry.

Sobriety was an eye-opener; no pun intended. It also led to the resurrection of my writing career, which would subsequently include two Pulitzer Prize nominations and the publication of this, my fifth book. The best part, though, is I've been sober ever since.

There but for the grace of God, and many caring friends, I'd be John Belushi.

My 2005 book, *Our Brother's Keeper*, told of my younger brother Jeff's 1968 death while serving with the Marine Corps in Vietnam and how his death led to my out-of-control alcohol addiction and, eventually, to the struggle to maintain sobriety. As part of ongoing treatment, Brawner's doctors and psychiatrists insisted I distance myself from all drinking buddies and the free-wheeling, around-the-clock manic lifestyle. Sounds easy enough except...I had no friends who didn't drink. And I was possessed by my job as the Sunday Sports Editor at the *Atlanta Journal-Constitution*.

Possessed because our sports section was the nation's premier entity. Due to alcoholism plus the way I am wired, maintaining excellence has always been a matter of life and death to me. I approached each week as if going to war, taking no prisoners.

I was my worst enemy.

Way the shrinks put it, I was on a never-ending merry-go-round in constant pursuit of perfection, which was always just out of reach. By never letting my foot up off the gas, everything around me was a maddening blur, thus making it impossible for me to see what was less than a mile down the road — death. The only way to maintain sanity and sobriety was to abandon ship. I must walk away from my friends, seek a career change, and wholeheartedly embrace AA.

All I'd done for the previous 14 years was live and breathe sports and wash down the pain with a bottle of Guinness. Now, in the blink of an eye, I was being denied both. I was a man without a country. An outcast, even if it was voluntary.

Hardest thing I ever did. Hardest thing I've continued to do.

However, the *AJC* always had my back. Once I explained what it would take for me to maintain sobriety, they moved me to the Lifestyle Department where I became the assistant editor in charge of helping design its daily section. Mainly, I just kept my head down and stayed out of other people's way. That move certainly helped reduce my anxiety and paranoia. Still, for the longest time I felt as if I had a sign on my back declaring I was an insane Irishman carrying around the misdeeds of his past.

I had become that hated of all things: a cliché.

The best part of the move to Lifestyle, though, was it offered an opportunity to occasionally write. Hell, as a functioning drunk, I could've done the design job in my sleep. But I felt pigeonholed being known as a great designer and it was sapping my soul. To live life to the fullest, I needed to write. My sobriety depended on it. So, whenever the opportunity arose to hone that craft, I attacked it with passion, working on stories other reporters declined. Doing so on *my* time, *my* off-days, *my* vacation — and at *my* expense.

While I proved I could report and write as well as anyone, whatever pressure I experienced was self-induced. All I had to do was not give up. Not surrender. Hold fast to an adage that had been pounded into every fiber of my being —

Improvise!

Adapt!

Overcome!

Ooh-rah!

The first story I worked on was *The Road to Spotsylvania*. How I came to that story is next in this book. After weeks of research, I approached Mary Ellen Pettigrew, the managing editor of the *AJC's* prestigious *Atlanta Weekly* magazine, telling her I was in possession of an extraordinary cache of Civil War letters by a local Confederate soldier he had written to his wife and family. In that I had a week's vacation coming to me, would she be interested in a story set in the various battlefields the soldier described in his letters?

She thought the idea had merit.

When I showed her a couple of the letters, her eyes brightened. Yet, she still wasn't completely sold on the idea. Instead of pleading, I played my trump card. I'd be working on my own dime and on my own time.

And by the way, thanks for the opportunity, ma'am.

Mary Ellen approved the story but with precise conditions. While she liked the idea of blending history and the brutal course of the war detailed in the letters, I was to write succinct and to the point, keeping flowery prose to a minimum. When I mentioned I'd also be trying to locate the soldier's grave, she wasn't interested in whatever emotional ups and downs that search might involve. Instead, just stick to the letters and battlefields, she said; write a concise story about that journey.

Which I dutifully did. A fellow newspaper buddy of mine said, much to his chagrin, "Can't believe you're doing this for nothing."

But what the hell — nothing ventured, nothing gained, right?

I was burned out from designing pages and felt smothered. Writing was like stepping out into the sunshine. All I needed was to have a door opened so I could step through. Without doubts I believed *The Road to Spotsylvania*, even with its limited parameters, was the vehicle which would lead to a better tomorrow. It simply was a matter of having faith in something that was bigger than myself.

Mary Ellen loved the finished product, then surprised me with a $300 check. Whoa, never saw that coming, but again *Thank you, ma'am.*

Of greater importance, *AJC* Executive Editor Jim Minter also loved the story. He saw something in me others were quick to dismiss. Five months later he would send me off to cover my brother Marines in Beirut, Lebanon. One story in particular, *Christmas in a Combat Zone*, resulted in my first Pulitzer nomination.

All because of a mighty leap of faith in myself and yes, the Almighty Hand of Blessed Providence — once I was finally living a sober life.

The next chapter is the version of *The Road to Spotsylvania* I wanted to write but couldn't. The story behind the story. Complete with all the emotional twists and turns and tears of gratitude.

It holds a special place in my heart because, by refusing to be held hostage by the career dictates of others, I fought the good fight. Living this new life on my own terms, clean and sober, and doing what I've always done best — wearing my heart on my sleeve.

I hope you enjoy it as much I benefited from writing it.

1983

The Road to Spotsylvania

Edith Harbin, a gray-haired, prayerful Southern Belle of advanced age, came up to me at church one day in February. Aware of my journalistic success, she'd heard from another parishioner that I was also a military historian specializing in the Civil War. Edith said she was the great-grand-daughter of a Confederate soldier who, at 46, left his wife and their five children to defend his invaded country, dying in battle three years later in Virginia.

At that time of my life, going to church was a forced event and I was in a hurry to get out of there. But I stopped thinking about that immediately when she brought up the Holy Grail of the Civil War.

"I was wondering if you'd be interested in reading some letters he wrote to his wife and children back home in Cumming?"

She reached into her purse for a dainty handkerchief and dabbed at the tears flooding her eyes. With head bowed, she took a deep breath. "Josiah made his way to Atlanta. Volunteered on the Fourth of July of 1861. That was the last time his kin laid eyes on him. They were told that Josiah died at Spotsylvania in 1864. He was wounded on May 12, then shot a second time as he was being carried away on a litter. That second bullet is what killed him.

"Yes, Josiah Blair Patterson," Edith proudly stated, tears ceasing to flow. "He was a 1st Lieutenant in Company E, 14th Georgia Volunteer Infantry Regiment, Army of Northern Virginia. We've always assumed he was buried on the battlefield or thereabouts — somewhere in Virginia. But none of the family has ever been up there to see for themselves. Guess you'd say we're homebodies. We're Georgians; have been forever."

Edith paused, eyes pleading, tearing up, then said, "What is truly bothersome is that we've never known whether Josiah had himself a proper burial. We'd truly like to know."

Before I could react, she handed me a small box containing 34 letters, plus a wartime photo of Josiah in uniform he'd sent home. And then Edith Harbin solemnly and slowly departed, making her way back home to Norcross. Leaving whatever transpired next to be determined by my conscience and journalistic instincts. Besides, how could I say no to an old lady's tears — and Civil War letters?

The first letter of Josiah's that I pulled from the bunch was the succinct description of his regiment's part in the epic May 2 flanking assault at Chancellorsville against Union Gen. Joseph Hooker's Army of the Potomac. This surprise attack, the inspiration of Gen. Stonewall Jackson, continues to be studied at the National War College at Fort Lesley J. McNair, Washington, D.C.

> **May 8, 1863, Camp near Fredericksburg, Va.**
> I am now writing in great haste. My face is as yet unwashed, my hair uncombed. We took up line of march as

```
soon as we were relieved
from the front and taking a
circuitous route on
Saturday night, we were
again in line of battle
about two hundred yards
removed from the enemy.
Sabbath morning about
sunrise the ball opened in
earnest and the battle
raged with great fury until
about twelve o'clock. Our
regiment was the first to
break the enemy's line and
enter his works. Our
casualties amounted to
seventy-seven.
```

I was hooked. Through a dead man's words, Civil War history — what Southerners still call The War Between the States and others call The War of Northern Aggression — came alive with the dullness of camp life, the marches of the army, and the death and destruction on the battlefield.

The decision to help Edith was easy. Bill Parker, a friend of mine from the *Chicago Tribune*, had already planned to visit in May. A fellow historian, we'd previously laid the groundwork for a Civil War excursion through Virginia and onward to Gettysburg. He'd do the driving, we'd split expenses. I called Parker and told him about Lt. Patterson's letters and the battles he'd participated in. He was all for it. Following the Confederate soldier's war journey was a no-brainer. I couldn't believe my good fortune.

I telephoned Edith. Told her I was going to look further into her great-grandfather's war exploits, scouring any local historical records I might come across. And then I would eventually travel to Virginia in hopes of possibly locating his grave.

Her tears were joyful.

I thanked her for trusting me with the letters and turned back to reading.

> **July 12, 1862**
> **Camp near Richmond, Va.**
> *I feel that I belong to my country, that if my wife and daughter were but men, they, too, would be by my side bravely defending their insulted and invaded country. I feel that in acting I have but proven myself to be worthy of their love and affection.*

With those warrior's words for the ages, I was inspired to retrace Lt. Patterson's footsteps with the Army of Northern Virginia and vicariously experience the thunder of the guns and the cries of the wounded from Seven

Pines to Chancellorsville, from Gettysburg to Spotsylvania. It would be a journey of transformation.

One where Patterson came alive, his words took form. Where he no longer merely represented harshly inked scrawls on faded pieces of parchment.

To prepare for this part of the trip, I visited Georgia's Department of Archives & History and made Xerox copies of the Descendants Roll Call of the 14th Georgia Volunteer Infantry Regiment. It confirmed, in concise script:

> Patterson, Josiah B., 2nd Lieutenant July 4, 1861; Elected 1st Lieutenant, November 8, 1862; Killed at Spotsylvania, Virginia, May 12, 1864. Buried there.

Those last two words gave me hope of fulfilling Edith Harbin's request.

Once again studying Lt. Patterson's photo, taken in Richmond during the autumn of 1863, it seemed to tell a story of its own. Both he and the cause for which he fought had lost much of their luster by then. Robert E. Lee's Army of Northern Virginia had suffered a crushing defeat a month earlier at Gettysburg. There is nothing elegant about Patterson's nondescript butternut uniform; the wear and tear on it spoke volumes about the suffering he and his fellow warriors had during two long and turbulent years at the hands of Federal forces.

It was a far cry from the summer of 1861 when war erupted. The grand illusion of battle was first shattered on the grassy plains alongside the meandering stream called Bull Run. The pomp, the glory of men at arms, died among the flame and fire of rifled cannon on July 21, 1861.

Although the 14th Georgia had enlisted too late for the war's initial confrontation, Patterson was able to get a firsthand glimpse of war's horrific remnants.

November 24, 1861

near Manassas

Carcasses lie thick upon its surface and bones lie bleaching and enriching the soil. Man and beasts here mingle in dust and the forest around bears evidence of the hard-fought field.

It was time to contact the chief historian at Fredericksburg & Spotsylvania National Military Park. I identified myself as a reporter for the *Atlanta Journal-Constitution* and the particulars of the story I was working on. He politely informed me of the difficulties ahead because at least sixty-seven percent of the war's estimated 620,000 Union and Confederate dead were buried under headstones marked "Unknown".

Further dampening my hopes, at war's end in April 1865, the U.S. Congress authorized the establishment of a national cemetery at Fredericksburg to provide a proper burial place for Union soldiers who died there, plus those Federal troops killed at the three other major battles within a 20-mile radius of Fredericksburg (including Chancellorsville, the Wilderness, and Spotsylvania). Finding the grave of a particular Confederate soldier of the 1500 killed during the horrendous May 1864 fighting at Spotsylvania might prove to be impossible.

The chief historian said, "I think what you're trying to accomplish has a noble quality to it. I'll do some research for you. Who knows? Providence will maybe smile upon you."

In May 1983, Bill Parker and I embarked on a quest I now was beginning to view as a fool's errand, the Hand of Providence or not.

Nonetheless, the words of a fellow warrior, a long-dead lieutenant, compelled me to press forward.

Holding tight to an adage pounded into my Marine soul —Improvise! Adapt! Overcome! — I immersed myself in Patterson's letters describing his first taste of battle at Seven Pines to Frayer's Farm and Gaines' Mill, and finally his last letter, composed in the shadow of a war lost:

June 13, 1862
Camp on Chickahominy

I have never spent a more miserable night in my life. We had to wade a large pond of water to reach the enemy. This pond was filled with fallen timber logs, treetops, bushes, and the water was up to the hips. Darkness closed the fight, said to be the severest of this revolution. The cries and moaning of the wounded were heard long after nightfall. Our company was scattered here and there. Rumor said we were cut to pieces. Cold, wet, languid, mourning my missing comrades, uncertain of their fate, I spent that night after the battle of Seven

Pines. May God preserve me from another night like that.

July 12, 1862
Camp near Richmond, Va.

On Thursday the 26th June we crossed the Chickahominy at Meadow Bridge, a dangerous and hazardous enterprise, but the success of our forces in repelling McClellan depended upon our turning his right flank at Mechanicsville. About four o'clock we made the assault, our Regt. being the first to engage the enemy in connection with the Louisiana Battalion and the 35th Georgia. Darkness closed the fight. [The next day] we advanced about one mile beyond Gaines Mill.

Shell and shot began to rain upon our midst. From that till night the battle raged. Gen. Lee said such fighting had no precedent. We again held the field and camp of the enemy. On Saturday we stopped to take care of wounded and to bury the dead.

February 26, 1864
from Richmond, Va.

I cannot agree with those who cry out that we are whipped…the enemy offers no terms of peace that do not bring dishonor and degradation in their train. Our all depends upon the continuance of the struggle…The army is a unit. It needed no legislation to force it to its highest duty. It

> *has offered its services*
> *a free will offering. It*
> *is for the War, long or*
> *short. War to the knife*
> *and the knife to the*
> *hilt. God grant us*
> *success.*

Less than three months later Gen. U.S. Grant's vast Army of the Potomac methodically pushed Lee's dwindling force back toward Richmond. Josiah Patterson would die before the Union guns at Spotsylvania on May 12.

Almost 119 years to the day, I found myself standing on the very ground near which Patterson was killed. A tiny corner of Hell within the remnants of a vast Confederate trench system that came to be known as the Bloody Angle.

I'm standing in a steady downpour, cold, soaked to the bone. Just as were the combatants that dismal day when

20,000 Union soldiers stormed this flawed portion of the Rebel trench system, which jutted out toward the enemy like an extended fist, exposing it to murderous crossfire.

It prompted survivor John Haley of the 17th Maine to describe the ensuing 22 hours of nonstop fighting as "a seething, bubbling, roaring hell of hate and murder". Echoing the sentiment, a Confederate survivor described the carnage as a "boiling, bubbling and hissing caldron of death".

On this rainy day, though, all that is missing is the maniacal chaos, incessant gunfire, horrific screaming, and the rivulets of free-flowing blood. Allowing my imagination to take control, I felt numb. For once Lee's battered army retreated toward the North Anna River the following day. Rather than digging individual graves for their enemy, Union burial teams found it easier to simply collapse this section of trenchworks, entombing an unknown number of Confederate dead — many of whom lay piled four and five deep amid mud and blood-stained water below.

I shivered and wondered if, indeed, Lt. Josiah Patterson's remains lay buried somewhere beneath the undulating terrain at my feet.

A possibility, for park rangers back at the Fredericksburg & Spotsylvania Battlefield Visitors Center had earlier informed me they had found no record of Patterson's burial.

Having checked the roster of identified burials at Fredericksburg's City Cemetery, where the Ladies Memorial Association of Fredericksburg had purchased a plot of land in 1867 for a Confederate cemetery, Patterson was not listed among 3553 of mostly unknown Southern soldiers re-interred there.

I hurried to the warmth of Parker's vehicle and did my best to dry off. It was a somber moment, for I knew my journey had come to an end. I had not found the grave I sought. What was I going to tell Edith? I've never accepted failure gracefully, so my heart and gut ached on the nine-mile drive back to Fredericksburg. Windshield wipers barely keeping up with the rain rhythmically heightened the disappointment.

Mission unaccomplished, yet nonetheless grateful for the time and energy the park rangers had expended seeking a touch of closure for Josiah Patterson's relatives.

What would happen next, to this very day, still seems like a schmaltzy ending from a movie like *Field of Dreams* or *Rudy*. Unbelievable. Corny. Sentimental. Then again, who am I to complain? All that was missing were the haunting strains of *The Bonnie Blue Flag* because Providence indeed was with me this day.

Upon arrival at Fredericksburg, one of the rangers approached and said they'd overlooked a small private cemetery that was not part of the park system and off the beaten path outside of Spotsylvania. Back in the day, he said, a group of local ladies, obviously concerned about the number of unattended and crudely marked graves scattered about the battlefield, formed the Spotsylvania Memorial Association.

An ear-to-ear smile could not hide the ranger's joy. "Those ol' ladies formed this memorial group in 1866, establishing the Confederate Cemetery on five acres of land a half-mile northeast of Spotsylvania Courthouse. Best part is, of the remains of 570 Confederate soldiers buried there, almost all of 'em are identified. Now, I can't say as if the gentleman you're looking for is there or not, on account no one that we know of seems to have a record of the names. Can't hurt none for us to go and see for ourselves, right?"

With that, Parker and I accepted a ride in the Ranger's vehicle and off we went, south on Lafayette Boulevard and Route 208 for about nine miles in a steady downpour, then slowed as we reached the Spotsylvania Battlefield tour road exit.

"Cemetery's 'bout a half-mile up here on our left," the Ranger said, unable to control his excitement. "Who knows, with any luck, your soldier's remains mighta been carried off the battlefield, laid to rest up the road here."

Held my breath as he slowed and turned left onto a shrubbery-lined gravel road that ended before brick pillars supporting a black, cast-iron arch reading Confederate Cemetery. I remember staring at the arch for the longest time, saying nothing, as the rain suddenly ceased, and the sun burst brightly through the clouds.

"Graves are partitioned by state," the Ranger said, identifying the plots which would be on my left as I entered the cemetery as belonging to North Carolina, Virginia, Mississippi, Tennessee, Arkansas, and Texas, the headstones of which were provided by the Federal government.

"From what I've been told, as you swing 'round that monument of the Confederate soldier standing guard over this hallowed ground, you'll come across the Louisiana section, then South Carolina and Alabama. Those Georgia boys are the first section on your right."

Down the gravel walkway into the cemetery I went and momentarily paused in front of the concrete block marker at my feet identifying this as the final resting place for 63 Georgians, plus 21 unknown Confederate soldiers, all aligned in seven rows.

Without a moment's hesitation, I unconsciously made way to Row 4.

Turned, and in a daze, carefully stepped past the first 10 graves.

And then kneeled in front of the greatly weathered, mildew-stained headstone inscribed Lt. Josiah B. Patterson, 14th GA INF, CSA.

Afterward, Parker and the Ranger joked about me having known all along where Lt. Patterson was buried. Surely, I'd been to this cemetery before, right?

"I mean, you didn't even spend any time searching," said Parker. "Just walked in and knelt at his grave."

I didn't know how to respond. Unable to admit it felt as if this entire journey had been preordained by the hand of an unfamiliar source. So, I kept my silence, filled with wonder.

Numb and embarrassed, for back at that old soldier's grave there had been no holding back my tears. Washed over with gratitude to that unseen yet powerful force that created the stunning revelation. Already anticipating the jubilation that would take place days later back home in Georgia among Josiah's extended relatives.

Most of all, foreseeing the tears of Edith Harbin's spiritual relief, knowing her great-grandfather had indeed been laid to rest in dignified fashion.

All of which is why, among the hallowed dead of gallant warriors of a long-lost cause, I had prayed a simple soldier's prayer: Thank you, Lord, for reminding us that not a sparrow falleth to the ground without your knowledge, Father — that not only are the hairs of our head numbered, but also remembered for eternity.

And then I rose and turned away. Moments later, the clouds closed once again, and rain swept over the cemetery at Spotsylvania.

LT. JOSIAH PATTERSON

Country music legend Willie Nelson's fortunes took a hit in 1989, as Big Brother let it be known that the ol' Outlaw was in arrears to the IRS to the tune of $16.7 million in back taxes. Though not necessarily cryin' in the rain, Willie embarked on an extensive nationwide tour, concentrating his efforts playing venues he had never before considered in order to settle his debt. He also tried his best to avoid interviews with the media.

As for myself, I continued looking for a place to settle down, thus spending much of my time on the road again — leaving the Chicago Tribune *in August 1981 to become Sports Editor of the* Kansas City Times*, then departing in March 1982 to become Sunday Sports Editor of the* Atlanta Journal-Constitution. *Finally planted roots in suburbia, becoming the sports columnist for the* Gwinnett Daily News *in April 1989 — the best job I ever had.*

All of which brings us to a gorgeous Sunday afternoon in June 1989 when Willie Nelson performed a post-Braves-game concert before 15,698 enthusiastic fans at Atlanta-Fulton County Stadium. My assignment that day was to somehow get Willie to let the good times roll.

1989

"He's Ridin' an' Hidin' His Pain"

Can't remember exactly how long I'd been waiting. Knew it was more than an hour, probably closer to two. Long enough for my butt to become numb, resting as it was on the concrete curb of the paved semicircle road that went from right field all the way to left and beneath the outfield bleachers at the Atlanta-Fulton County Stadium, home of the Braves.

Full of anxiety, I chain-smoked. The wait was agonizing. Was I gonna miss out on the interview of a lifetime? Felt weird, too, like I was one of them creepy voyeurs watching the windows of the tour bus as figures inside kept flitting back and forth.

As time slipped away, I recalled the words of a favorite song of mine, written by Edith Lindeman, a gal in the newspaper business like me. She was the entertainment editor of Virginia's *Richmond Times-Dispatch*. Co-writer and composer Carl Stutz was a musician who worked as an accountant and high school mathematics teacher. The song was made famous twenty years after it was written by the very man I was waiting for — another redhead. So to make waiting easier, I sang it to myself.

> *The redheaded stranger*
> *from Blue Rock, Montana*
> *Rode into town one day*
> *And under his knees*
> *was a ragin' black stallion*
> *And walkin' behind was a bay*

The bus I was surveilling was The Honeysuckle Rose and the door had still not opened for my next story. So, I sang some more:

The redheaded stranger
had eyes like the thunder
And his lips, they were
sad and tight
His little lost love
lay asleep on the hillside
And his heart was heavy as night

Found myself hopin' the aged cowboy inside the bus didn't think I was a damn revenuer and was cursing missing this interview if he did think that. I started on the next verse:

Don't cross him, don't boss him
He's wild in his sorrow
He's ridin' an' hidin' his pain
Don't fight him, don't spite him
Just wait till tomorrow
Maybe he'll ride on again

Decided at that point in the chorus to attempt to rise above it all, work out the kinks in my aching knees and rub a bit of circulation into the tightened and numbed muscles of my buttocks, when the door of the bus opened and this *redheaded stranger* beckoned me closer.

"Hey, son, whatcha doin' out there?" he asked, his voice coarsely melodious.

Didn't feel compelled to lie, told him I was singing one of my favorite songs by my all-time favorite Outlaw. Which, as expected, caused him to hesitate, then erupt into a broad smile and inquire, "You wouldn't by chance be a-waitin' for me, now would ya?"

Couldn't help but grin as I nervously stepped forward. Checked my watch, saw it was almost 4 o'clock, and said, "Your PR guy said to be here early, sir, so as not to take up too much of your time. What with you needin' to be ready for the concert and all."

Damned if that redheaded stranger didn't shake his head in disgust. "Well, he didn't say nothin' to me about it, so I reckon you're due an apology, son. C'mon in and..." He paused and cocked his head a bit, then clarified the invitation. "You ain't from the IRS, now are ya?"

Laughing, I said, "Hell, Willie, I'm bettin' I hate them bastards about as much as you do."

With that, Willie Nelson agreed to reminisce a bit, in essence trading all of his tomorrows for just one more yesterday...

And so, our tale begins in earnest with Willie giving his public relations dude a sharp rebuke, saying, "This reporter...uh, it's Jedwin, right? Now

Jedwin and me are gonna be talkin' for a while, hear? Won't be no bother. He's laid out the parameters — he's a-writin' a 'Willie Nelson, sports fan' story. Yep, and I'm a-likin' it already."

So went the next 40 minutes, the two of us sitting across from each other separated by a plate overflowing with fried chicken. No songs. No lyrics. No wild and wired words. No spirited high times, either. Just small talk of sports and life's extra-inning games — the tie-breakers and sudden deaths, skulled iron shots, birdies, and bogeys, missed extra points, and hitting the long ball off the wall for extra bases.

"I was a shortstop (at Abbott High School in Central Texas)," he said with a burst of soft-throated laughter, IRS demons exorcised momentarily from his consciousness at the same time. Also was a halfback on the Abbott football team, a guard on the basketball team, plus ran track. And in his spare time, was playing guitar in honky-tonks at age 13 and picking cotton in the summer through his senior year in high school.

"Almost got a scholarship to Weatherford Junior College. That's (25 miles west of Fort Worth) in Texas, you know. Shortstop, that was me. Getting balls hit at me going 90 miles-per-hour. One hot spot, that it was."

He paused, those memories bringing forth a burst of laughter. "Yes, I almost got a scholarship. Almost..."

Instead, he joined the Air Force in 1950, got married for the first time and, after completing his duty, drifted from one job to another — writing songs with no success, trimming trees, fashioning saddles, selling Bibles and vacuum cleaners door to door. "Just gettin' by," he says with a shrug.

We both reached for more chicken, munchin' away as his PR man fretted, constantly studying his wristwatch. Me, signaling time-out to make sure the tape recorder was working, my notetaking merely a backup. Am looking at those notes as I write this in 2020, wishing I'd thought to have him autograph 'em for posterity — the pages still bearing swaths of grease from the chicken.

Geezus. Where was my brain?

Then Willie picked up the pace, elaborating on games and line drives heading his way, of sharp bouncers careening off the grass and up toward his heavily lined face — compliments of that harsh South Texas sun. Speakin' of good plays and good hits and defending one's self against life's high inside pitches. Yep, ol' Willie Nelson.

Sports Fan.

My, my; imagine that.

And, as expected, his thoughts were darting all over the place, but mostly on the road again...and those blue eyes were a-dancing with joy. There was nothing fake or phony about this conversation, mind you. It was obvious from the outset that this weathered music legend was enjoying himself, interrupting the flow from time to time by saying, "Sports, huh? Can you believe it?"

Laughing aloud and adjusting that red bandanna of his, recalling all those youthful yesterdays with a throaty chuckle, which said it all: Gee, ain't it funny how time slips away.

Pleasant reminiscences — singing gospel music at the local church; playing guitar in the local Bohemian Polka band at age nine; a few years later singing in dance halls and taverns, hopin' to catch a streak of lightning while emulating his favorite singers Hank Williams, Bob Wills, and Lefty Frizzell. With little success.

Still just gettin' by.

"Well, you gotta understand that my heroes were always Doak Walker and Bobby Layne, both Texas boys. Doak, a halfback for Southern Methodist University, winning the Heisman Trophy in 1948; and Bobby an All-American quarterback for the University of Texas," he said. "As a child, can't begin to tell you how many times I'd be listenin' to that radio and hearin' Doak a-runnin' and Bobby a-passin' for those touchdowns."

Pausing in quiet contemplation. "Yes, sir — a big sports fan, that's me."

Not to run afoul of one of his biggest-selling songs (*Mamas Don't Let Your Babies Grow Up To Be Cowboys* from the 1980 soundtrack of *The Electric Horseman*), he is also a big fan of Don Meredith, Charlie Waters, D.D. Lewis, and Bob Lilly — yes, indeed, his heroes have always been Cowboys. Old ones, mind you. Those out of Dallas, not

Austin. And if not Cowboys, then golfers — those who make the artful drives and avoid the hazards and sand traps, on and off the course.

I'm sitting across from him, studying his eyes and their earnestness, seeing those wrinkles in his face contort with that ever-present smile, thinking how most folks have got it all wrong — them contending that Willie Nelson is much closer to death than life. Couldn't be further from the truth, hear? He's 56, yet possesses the soul of a teenager, and is quick to say, "Why, son, it is the pursuit of sports that lets what little time I have slip away."

To which he deftly moves to his love affair with golf. More to the point, he's a self-admitted addict of it.

"Got my own course back home," which is just outside of Austin, right next to the fairways on the Pedernales

River — "which runs smack through LBJ country, you know."

The course is down to earth, he said, which describes the man himself.

"Anyway, I set my own par on that course," he says, chuckling at the irony of the admission. "Yep, I set my own par on every hole, every day." And when I ask what he shoots, he says, "Can't believe anything I say, son. Onaccounta I lie a lot."

Golf is Willie's release. And the company he keeps on life's not-so-fairways — Doug Sanders and Arnold Palmer and, yes, Lee Trevino, who "sure can talk your ear off, son" — anyway, these golf buddies keep the strain of his musical life from taking its expected toll.

"See, I'm not that real serious about the game, you know. Like, I don't let it get me sick if I don't play well. Some people, now, they live and die on the sport. That's why I could never be a professional. Why? Because those guys can't afford to skull one. Now me, I can. Figure there's always another shot up there somewhere."

A pause.

"You know, life is a game."

To which I respond: If that's the case, then you're a player of unparalleled perfection. Which he surely liked.

He also got a kick out of the sports analogy passed his way — this, between bites of chicken and plentiful bursts of easygoing laughter — how he is the Nolan Ryan of music, not just the country variety. How, as age keeps a-creepin' up on him, the music only gets better and better.

"That's good," Willie says, a complete stranger placing him shoulder-to-shoulder with the Texas Rangers' legendary Hall of Fame pitcher.

Admitting, even though the observation may be a bit unusual, it is yet somehow quite appropriate.

"Anyway, even though I have been playing this guitar since I was six...well, it does seem like I've been doing it a lifetime. But it was late in life before I really attained any measure of success. I mean, ol' Nolan had it all along."

Indeed.

But, still, Willie Nelson is batting close to a thousand over the past 14 years, ever since he recorded the album *Red Headed Stranger* in 1975. Yes, he's been on an enviable hitting streak ever since. Moving to Austin and embracing the burgeoning hippie music scene.

Growing the beard and mustache.

Wearing that red bandanna.

Hookin' up with Waylon Jennings and creating what came to be known as "Outlaw Country".

Appearing in movies.

Performing before presidents and other heads of state.

In short, becoming an American institution of sorts — rather than being confined to one.

Yep, not too many people can lay a glove on that, he says, again laughing softly. Then speaking of another love, jogging. How the leisurely daily runs have added years to his life. Added enjoyment, too, although, "Can't say as if the running has made the songs any better, but I sure can sing louder."

Then, in a voice one decibel above a whisper, "Even so, I still have my good days and my bad."

Nonetheless, as his PR manager once again hovered over our shoulders, pointing out the Braves game had concluded, the stage was set up and his family band was ready to strum a few tunes, and how all his fans were patiently waiting for his grand entrance,

Willie wasn't leaving without making one everlasting, parting statement:

"Son, I've been on the front pages, the business pages, the police pages, and the society pages. But I can't say as if I've ever been on the sports pages. So, I just wanna thank you. This has been relaxin', a whole lotta fun."

With that, we shook hands before taking separate paths to what we did best. Me, letting my readers know my heroes have always been cowboys; Willie taking center stage, entertaining as only he can, and singing some old, sweet songs…with Georgia on his mind.

JERRY GLANVILLE

1990

Sunday's Mournin' Coming Down

Jerry Glanville rode into our lives on that hallowed mid-day — January 14, 1990. Couldn't confirm if his drive that day was on his Harley or in his tricked-out '51 Mercury.

Was sure of the hour, though. High noon on a Sunday, it was. Yes, indeed… yet he'd opted not to show up in his usual cowboy attire. Expecting Gary Cooper, we got a disappointing Corporate America, what with him sporting a coat and tie and all.

No big black hat. No high plains drifter jacket. But softly humming "don't let the bastards get you down", a refrain from his good buddy Kris Kristofferson. And, yes, doing so while flashing that ever-present smartass grin that always seems to drive wussified folk in my profession apoplectic as well as infuriating the hell out of his serious NFL colleagues — especially the staid Steelers' Chuck Noll and Cincinnati's Sam Wyche.

Jerry Glanville always had a way with words, not to mention a brutal brand of football which not only produced victories but generated a fistful of enemies both on and off the playing field.

That he could instill pride in this team-oriented sport, lifting ailing franchises to playoff-level heights, was a given. He'd proven his worth as the Falcons' defensive coordinator (1979-

82), fashioning a helmet-cracking aggravated assault known as the "Gritz Blitz", which helped lead Atlanta to the playoffs during the 1980 and '82 seasons. And he'd produced the same results most recently (1985-89) as head coach of the Houston Oilers.

Yet, despite leading the Oilers to the playoffs for the third straight year, Glanville figured it was time for a more meaningful challenge. A few days earlier, he'd dropped the hint: "If you're not sleeping in Atlanta, you're just camping out."

And now here he was. In the flesh. An alleged renegade. Someone I knew only by his greatly flawed reputation. Helped explain the uncomfortable silence in the room. As Rankin Smith Sr., the Atlanta Falcons' owner, introduced the team's new head coach to the media gathered at the franchise's

Suwanee Complex, the air was thick with curiosity and restrained contempt.

Facing that, Glanville stood proud and self-assured. Grinnin' and brimmin' with optimism.

I found that difficult to comprehend. Mainly because he now held the reins of a gimpy, broken-down, and decrepit old nag of a professional football franchise that had become the NFL's redheaded stepchild over the past seven years — including three inept seasons under recently departed head coach Marion Campbell and the prior four seasons under Dan Henning.

Bottom line: If the franchise were a horse, it would have been mercifully put out of its misery long ago.

I was in attendance at the press conference, banished to the leper's section in the back of the room due to my big mouth. Not exactly blackballed, yet ostracized and publicly detested, nonetheless about as much as the gentleman about to address us.

As Glanville spoke, I reminisced how we'd arrived at this moment...

Twice Marion Campbell had served as head coach of the Falcons. He took up space for part of three seasons back in 1974-76, winning six games, losing 19, before being fired by then-general manager Pat Peppler.

Campbell didn't wait to be fired the second time around. Opted for an honorable exit with four games remaining in the '89 season. He retired after the team's 27-7 blowout at the hands of the hapless New York Jets on November 26.

How Campbell lasted as long as he had was baffling. He was a grumbling, age-old curiosity. Jurassic, in a modern-day sense. A crank-starting Model A

Ford in a world of slick, high-powered Shelby Mustang GT350s. In fact, Campbell had the distinction of being a three-time loser of winged creatures, doing disservice to the Philadelphia Eagles (1983-85) between two Falcon flights of incompetence. All told, teams under his misguidance won 34 games, lost 80, with one tie — to this day the fifth-lowest winning percentage among those who have coached at least five seasons in the NFL.

Which left me wondering: Did he possess incriminating photographs?

As the newly hired sports columnist for the *Gwinnett Daily News*, I first met Campbell on the opening day of the Falcons' 1989 training camp. He had the charisma of a sloth. I covered the team's first seven games (only two were won), and patiently waited for any of the numerous beat reporters or columnists from other media outlets to at least hint at what I knew needed to be said: For the good of the team and its long-suffering fans, the Falcons' brass should fire Campbell.

Without hesitation.

Pull the trigger.

Now.

But nary a discouraging word was heard. It was as if the guys and gals on Press Row had become immune to despicable football.

As to why I hesitated to raise my own voice? I plead indifference. I was the new guy on the block, the rookie columnist, the well-traveled sports reporter from Illinois, Florida, Wisconsin, and Missouri. Sure, I'd covered the Bears, Packers, Dolphins, Bucs, and Chiefs. But what did I know about Falcons? Lame birds were not my specialty. So, I maintained my silence through Atlanta's horrific 2-5 start. And unlike the rest of the sporting mob, I am a recovering alcoholic, thus didn't need the luxury of inundating myself with copious amounts of booze to wash away the horrors I'd seen on the playing field.

Sobriety does have its advantages.

Once the inept Arizona Cardinals got done dismantling the Falcons 34-20 on October 22, 1989, I'd reached my offensive-retching limit. Having had a bellyful of football futility, the column I wrote four days later was downright damning. Lest anyone miss the points I made in the column, here is a handy bulleted list of all it condemned in Campbell. His:

- lack of leadership
- business acumen
- entrepreneurship
- motivation
- and innovation

His Falcons were prop-driven relics in an age of supersonic jets. As such, I stunned the Falcons' brass and my peers by writing that Campbell should be shown the door with the promise he never darken it again.

Prior to voicing that opinion, though, I'd faithfully followed the shrink's advice. Pausing for a deep breath before placing Campbell between the crosshairs of my journalist gunsight, I took a closer look at the organization before squeezing the trigger.

The front office was top notch, and the team itself — from Deion Sanders to Scott Case, Chris Miller, and Mike Kenn — was at least several notches removed from the mediocrity it displayed.

Nonetheless, there was no fire in the team's belly.

"Inept commanders order men into battle; the successful ones choose to lead their men into harm's way," a highly decorated combat veteran and Falcon fan told me. "As for Marion Campbell? I wouldn't follow him down the hallway, let alone onto the football field."

So, four days after the Falcons' fifth lethargic loss, I wrote what no other member of Atlanta's media had the cojones to say: It was time for Atlanta to rid itself of Marion Campbell.

And just like that, you'd think I had the bubonic plague. I was an outcast among my colleagues, all of whom respected Campbell for his bull-necked pedigree. South Carolina born and bred. Star defensive lineman for the University of Georgia Bulldogs. Eight-year NFL veteran of the San Francisco 49ers and Philadelphia Eagles.

After all, he was one of us. A good ol' boy who'd done good. No harm, no foul, y'hear? Besides, Marion's not a bad person; loves his wife a bunch. Besides, them ol' gimpy-winged, choke-under-pressure Falcons have pretty much always been horse-droppings for as long as we can remember, right?

Anyway, while I simply brushed off what I considered to be institutional nonsense, I had to endure the stink-eye from my peers. Whenever I walked into Falcon headquarters or the press box on game days, it was as if I were Moses thrusting that shepherd's staff of his into the Red Sea. The maddened crowd parted. Making hasty retreats. In private, the players suddenly became RINOs: thought I'd made a gutsy call, but publicly stayed silent and kept a nice, solid distance.

That I was persona non grata is an understatement.

But I wasn't wrong in what I wrote.

Anyway, five games later, four of which were losses, Campbell could sense the foundation under his feet crumbling and chose to retire. Assistant coach Jim Hanifan took the ship's wheel for the remaining four games and steered the listing vessel onto the rocks. Just how irrelevant the team had become was reflected in the season finale at Atlanta-Fulton County Stadium, a 31-24 Christmas Eve loss to the Detroit Lions. Attendance at the season finale was a franchise-low of only 7,792.

Hell, local high school games drew bigger crowds.

Thus ended a horrific 3-13 season.

And now, twenty days later, "The City Too Busy to Hate" was getting the one coach who irritated the league's entire corporate structure. He dressed funny, what with those spiffy hand-crafted cowboy boots, big hat, *Top Gun* shades, and that Johnny Cash "Man in Black" attire. Besides that, Glanville was the proverbial burr under the saddle of the national media. He had a habit of irritating one and all.

Then again, when Glanville's critics couldn't stomach him, he'd simply grin and quip: "Well, hush my mouth, darlin'." Because if you didn't like him, he probably didn't like you first. Which sorta reminded me of myself.

So, why the contempt among the Fourth Estate?

For starters, Glanville preached a devil-be-damned, knock-their-jocks-off mayhem and happy-hand-grenade football. What he called "living life on the edge". A combative mindset that called for relentlessly attacking the enemy until you flat-out wore 'em down. A devil-be-damned style of play that left no room on his team for those who'd hesitate to make opposing running backs pay a painful price for carrying the football. In other words, thumb-suckers, folks who were "a-feared of shedding a bit of blood"…for the greater good, of course. (Geezus, sounds like certain so-called Republicans of late.)

Sports Illustrated once opined that Jerry Glanville had come to Atlanta with an Iwo Jima philosophy — insisting the flag be raised on every play. His specialty was a take-no-prisoners brand of bedlam. He was a steely-eyed, circuit-ridin', saddlebag preacher who converted his players into makin' the other SOBs pay dearly for denigrating whatever House of Pain or Shame Glanville was presently working in.

He had my blood pumpin'.

Ooh-rah!

Anyway, once Glanville had given his upbeat, inspirational best to the skeptical press corps — lots of "We're gonna come out fightin', kickin' butt, and takin' names," or words to that effect — he dutifully allowed questions, answering all in upbeat fashion.

And once all the tape recorders and TV cameras had been turned off, he looked around the room and asked, "Okay, which one of you characters is Jedwin Smith?"

Deadly silence followed in which one coulda heard an ant pass gas.

I was in the room's cheap seats, where I'd been relegated since hanging Campbell out to dry in print. Calmly easing my cowboy-booted feet to the ground, I arose and said, "Reporting for duty, SIR."

Glanville broke into a big grin, stepped down from the podium and made his way toward me. Face-to-face, nose-to-nose we were. Tension in the room palpable. My contemporaries were expecting the iron-fisted coach to maybe slap me upside the head or question the legitimacy of my birth —

you know, readin' me the riot act, laying down one of those "my-way-or-the-highway" sets of ground rules, remedying once and for all my rebellious behavioral disorders and put me in my place.

Instead, he immediately threw his arm around my shoulders, pulled me in close and, with a soft authoritative voice, said, "Once I took the job, the front office guys here told me I'd have no problems with any of the members of the media — except for you, that is. But I told 'em that you and me were gonna get along just fine, pawdna!"

He grabbed my right hand in a powerful grip, earnestly shook it, and said, "Yep, there's a new sheriff in town, son, and you and me are gonna be havin' ourselves a whole lotta fun."

And by God, we did.

Without doubt, the man knew how to generate excitement. He changed the team's uniforms from red to black, and installed the wide-open run-and-shoot offense. And in the blink of an eye, Falcon Fever swept through the city. Front office folks were overwhelmed by the number of newfound fans purchasing season tickets. And the product Glanville put on the field that first year suddenly was pretty much worth the price of admission.

Looking back at his 1990 inaugural 5-11 season, the record didn't say it all. His Falcons beat the team that had discarded him (those Oilers, a 47-27 blowout in the season-opener), plus clipping nemesis Sam Wyche's Bengals (another blowout, 38-17).

Seven of the team's losses were by a touchdown or less.

Mediocrity no longer resided at Atlanta-Fulton County Stadium. Attendance swelled to near-capacity. And damned if he didn't set the city on fire during his second season in 1991 with playoff-bound, "Back in Black", jaw-droppin' excitement executed with offensive and defensive fire and brimstone. The locker room atmosphere was raucous, no longer like a tomb in seasons past. Hip-hop music played at ear-splitting levels and celebrities led the celebrations with MC Hammer belting out his *U Can't Touch This* or the team's adopted *2 Legit 2 Quit* battle cry, then steppin' aside to make room for heavyweight champion Evander Holyfield, who wanted to personally congratulate Deion Sanders for another high-steppin' All-Pro performance.

What all this giddiness emphasized was the Falcons had elevated themselves to a 10-6 record, then stunned the New Orleans Saints 27-20 in the NFC wild-card game, the franchise's first playoff victory since 1978, before losing 24-7 in the NFC divisional playoffs to the eventual Super Bowl champion Washington Redskins.

Along the way, I became Glanville's shadow — Sancho Panza to his Don Quixote. One-hundred-plus-miles-per-hour jaunts on his Harley. Down in the pits at Lanier Speedway watching him test his skills racing in the NASCAR Busch Grand National Series. Relaxing with him during the playoffs in the lobby of a swank D.C. hotel, listening to Jerry Jeff Walker reminisce about his star-studded singing career.

Jerry, Jedwin, and Jerry.

Damn.

Can still hear Jerry Jeff a-strummin' and serenading us with the lyrics of *Mr. Bojangles* and *Up Against the Wall, Redneck Mother*…

Occasionally, we'd talk football. But Glanville knew that I knew his Falcons were light years from being Super Bowl champions. So we'd be chatting about undersized defensive end Tim Green's propensity to always play above his natural capabilities, or how, had safety Scott Case been born a century earlier, he would have been walking alongside Doc Holliday, Wyatt Earp, and Earp's brothers toward the O.K. Corral.

And before you could recite the opening verse of Waylon Jennings' *Good Ol' Boys* theme song from *The Dukes of Hazzard*, the conversation would turn to how both of us enjoyed the company of friends in low places.

Yep, Country music was our shared weakness. And because Jerry neither drank nor smoked, and what with me having embraced sobriety for almost eight years at the time, plus making sure I never fired up one of my Pall Malls in his presence, Glanville would laugh as he started relating tales about some of his favorite people: Jerry Jeff and Johnny Cash, Travis Tritt and Garth Brooks,

Willie Nelson and Waylon Jennings, and
Kris Kristofferson, whose *Sunday
Morning Coming Down* was one of the
coach's all-time favorites, especially one
line of the lyrics:

*Cause there's something in a Sunday
makes a body feel alone…*

Or we'd be passing the time of day
in his Suwanee office, me sharing how
my publisher at the *Gwinnett Daily News*
had to be talked out of firing me by the
rest of the *GDN* brass because I'd said in
a column how I wasn't a fan of
Washington, D.C., because Richard
"Tricky Dick" Nixon had slept there.

Damn, the ol' ball coach got a kick
out of that, then said I should borrow a
line from Travis Tritt and tell the
publisher "here's a quarter, call
someone who cares".

Indeed, Jerry Glanville's life story
oftentimes read like the lyrics of a

Kristofferson country tune, especially the likes of *The Pilgrim, Chapter 33*:

```
He's a walkin' contradiction,
       partly truth and
       partly fiction,
Takin' ev'ry wrong direction
on his lonely way back home...
```

But wins and losses, NFL playoffs, and that Country music swagger aside, what truly endeared the man to me transpired on a Thursday morning, November 14, in the aftermath of a telephone call from him during that inaugural 1990 season.

"Wanna take a helicopter ride with me?" he asked.

Having an aversion to transport choppers, I hesitated. He assured me no one would be shooting at us, so I agreed. Next thing I knew, we were zipping along at 180 miles per hour, skimming over Atlanta at 5000 feet in a

Lookey who came out to see Jedwin.

Travis Tritt,
Waylon Jennings,
& Jerry Glanville

massive Sikorsky 76 helicopter, en route to Scottish Rite Children's Medical Center. Why?

Because Glanville simply wanted to say hello to the kids.

Long before he arrived in Atlanta, this was a journey of faith and spiritual blessings he'd been making at other NFL ports of call in Detroit, Buffalo, and Houston. I was anticipating what we journalists scathingly call a "dog and pony show", a feel-good piece of scripted public relations theatrics orchestrated mainly by politicians and other cold-hearted individuals. Mainly, putting lipstick on a hog.

Having shadowed Glanville now for the past nine months, I should have known better. And the images that tugged at my heart that day still linger, even three decades later…

"Are you Jerry Glanville?" the nurse asks as she reaches out to touch the left elbow of the Falcons coach.

"Yes I am, darlin'," Glanville says with a soft smile.

"Could you please stop by to see Scott? He's one of my patients. It would really help him," the nurse says, her eyes pleading.

Scott used to be a safety on his school's football team. Today, he is flat on his back in room 417 in a building where, too often, youngsters are brought to die. With Scott, though, this isn't the case. He suffers from chronic headaches. His spirit is lagging. And on this day, his parents pray for a miracle.

Glanville approaches Scott's bed. The child's smile cuts through the darkness that normally hovers over these clinical surroundings.

"You're telling me you saw us against the Bengals?" Glanville asks as he reaches out and gently holds the youngster's right hand. "Well, pawdna, we won that game because of you. Do you believe that?"

Scott nods his head; his smile spreads from nurse to parents.

"I'll tell you what, Scott," Glanville says, his voice breaking, "we've gotta get you outta here so you can give us some more good luck. And another thing, son. You're a safety and I love safeties. Are you a hard hitter?"

Again, Scott nods his head. With tears in his eyes he says, "Yes, sir."

"Well, son, I love hard hitters. So I want you to fight the fight. If you do, you'll get well. And when you get well, I'm gonna buy you a milkshake when you get out of here," says Glanville as he gives Scott a Falcons ballcap.

The coach gently pats Scott's hand and hobbles out of the room on his damaged left knee from his college playing days. It's acting up again, but he says, "No room for my pain today."

Clay Callaway, the hospital's safety officer, leads us down the hall to room 414, where 10-year-old Kyle is being held prisoner by what doctors have diagnosed as a possible brain tumor. Kyle and his parents, originally from Pennsylvania, moved here only 10 weeks ago.

"Tell you what I'm gonna do, Kyle," Glanville says. "I'm gonna turn you into a Falcons fan."

The child says nothing. With eyes as big as silver dollars locked into those of Glanville, and after what seems like an eternity, Kyle smiles.

"Keep the faith. Keep fighting," the coach says. "And remember this — my prayers are for you. We love you, son."

Bryan, a teenager, has wires strapped to his chest while he valiantly clutches hope in two frail hands.

Nearby, an infant has tubes running into its neck.

Bed after bed is filled with the helpless. For some, life will end here in this hospital. For others, faith is carried on the wings of the strangest birds.

"Every Thursday, when my team breaks for lunch, I break for here," Glanville is saying as we make our way through the hospital corridors. "The greatest thing is you'll see a smile where the Doc says there hasn't been a smile in ten days."

Against a backdrop of caring doctors and sympathetic nurses, we walk in a world where the only screams are those from the heart because here, on the first floor, most of the children quietly endure their pain and discomfort, and others patiently await death.

"A mother wrote me recently," says Glanville, his eyes vacant as we move through the intensive care unit, "saying how her son loved me — not because I was a football coach, because her son really hated football, but because I prayed for her boy."

You wait for the punch line, dreading what you know you will hear. "Yeah," says the coach in a whisper, his eyes filling with tears. "Cancer. Died."

From room to room…

Past a father who pushes his child in a wheelchair. "You don't know it yet, coach, but this is your next halfback," says the proud father, who stops to shake Glanville's hand.

From room to room…

"We love you, too, Bryan," the coach says to another 10-year-old patient. "Our prayers are going out for you, son."

A couple doors away, an 11-year-old had to have all the bones in his chest broken to facilitate surgery. "I'll tell you what, Jason. When you get out of here, I want you standing with me on the sidelines."

Jason looks up at Glanville and cries, "It hurts so much, Coach."

From room to room…

James, age 12, oxygen mask strapped over his mouth. Grandmother at his side takes hold of the child's left hand and says: "This is Coach Glanville, James. He brought you a cap. He is praying for you, honey."

James opens his eyes and forces a smile. And then he, too, cries.

Outside the room, Glanville's voice again breaks, "If you look close enough, you see a lot of miracles."

Miles away from everyone's tears, our Sikorsky banks hard left and noses down onto the Falcons' practice field. The coach jokes about us "living on the edge" and how "you gotta be a little bit crazy to be a chopper pilot".

But our laughter is forced.

Not long ago, a high school hemophiliac contracted AIDS through a blood transfusion. In the words of Glanville, "The kid was an unbelievable student, an unbelievable athlete. Our whole goal was to get him to the [October 7th] home game against the Saints [a 28-27 victory], but he died the Thursday before the game. Somehow, I think he saw us win the game, though. In spirit, you know?"

We do. And we also know that when the young man was buried, he wore Glanville's black coaching jacket.

"You have experiences like that," Glanville says, his eyes following the helicopter as it lifts off for the return trip to downtown Atlanta, "and you realize why you have to keep going back to hospitals. Just think how much good you could accomplish if everyone just took one hour a week to stop by and say hello to the kids."

He pauses and, like everything else he does, says how these trips are a team effort; how Brenda Johnston, his secretary, and Carol Breeding, the Falcons' director of community relations, deserve all the credit.

"Yes, sir, if you do this often enough, you come to realize that you and me don't have any problems."

A few hours later, back at the *Gwinnett Daily News*, I received a telephone call from the mother of a child Jerry Glanville had visited that morning. Here is what she said:

"Mr. Smith, you and Mr. Glanville visited Scott this morning at Scottish Rite. I just wanted to tell you we have been waiting for a breakthrough for three weeks and two days for Scott. And y'all were a big issue in helping that come about today.

"Scott's whole motivation level has changed, and we've seen a tremendous difference in this boy. Just called to simply say thank you. You're doing more than you think. We're still here at Scottish Rite, but we hope to leave soon. Thank you so much."

It's been thirty years since I received that message, yet I still fight back the tears. And doing so, once again I'm reminded of something Jerry Glanville told me as we'd exited Scottish Rite Children's Medical Center on that long-ago day.

"This is done for the sake of the children," Glanville said. "What I don't want you to do is paint me out to be something I'm not. Sure, this is a life-changing experience. But I don't do it because I'm anything special. I probably get more out of it than the kids do."

Well, hush my mouth, darlin'.

POSTSCRIPT

Jerry Glanville's last stint in Atlanta lasted four seasons. That glorious second year high of reaching the NFL playoffs was followed by consecutive 6-10 seasons. The Falcons cut him loose in 1993, which explains why he's always said the NFL "stands for Not For Long".

He spent the next 10 years racing on the NASCAR and ARCA circuits, visiting our troops in a patriotic goodwill tour of Iraq, then working as an NFL analyst with HBO, CBS, and Fox, before returning to the college sidelines, first as a defensive coordinator at the University of Hawaii (2005-06), then head coach at Portland State (2007-09). He returned to the professional circuit in 2018 as a defensive coordinator for the Canadian Football League's Hamilton Tiger-Cats, then was hired (2020) as defensive coordinator for the Tampa Bay Vipers in the XFL.

Now, at 79, you'd think he would have finally come to the realization that it was time to step out of those fancy boots of his, put on a pair of slippers, and sit back and relax. But rocking chairs have never suited him. So, he's never more than an email or telephone call away, keeping in touch with close friends or letting it be known he has interest in another coaching gig.

After all, there's no holding the man back. He's one of those rare true believers, forever optimistic, always holding fast to the positive, his focus on a brighter tomorrow. Still contending "I've never had a bad day in my life" and never regretting having taken the reins of a broken-down nag of a football team "because the fun of the job is climbing out of the hole."

Yes, he's thoroughly enjoyed plenty of life's highs:

- Penned his own autobiography (*Elvis Don't Like Football* in 1990 with J. David Miller),
- Appeared in music videos with MC Hammer (*2 Legit 2 Quit* in 1992),
- And had cameos in movies (*Hoffa* with Jack Nicholson and Danny DeVito in 1992, and *The Last Movie Star* in

2017 with Burt Reynolds and Chevy Chase).

And on this particular day, coming to terms with the worst of life's lows. Presently mourning the loss of his good friend Jerry Jeff Walker, who died at age 78 the night before (October 23, 2020) after a long battle with throat cancer.

Says Glanville, "His death has made grown men cry. Love that man."

Other books by the author

Fatal Treasure

Our Brother's Keeper

Let's Get It On: The Mills Lane Story

I AM ISRAEL:
Lions and Lambs of the Land

BLUEROOMBOOKS.COM
blueroombooks@outlook.com
A MARINE and a JOURNALIST
WALK INTO A BAR
JEDWIN SMITH
978-1-950729-10-4

ISBN 13: 978-1-950729-10-4